Johanna Krause

TWICE PERSECUTED

Johanna Krause

TWICE PERSECUTED

Surviving in
Nazi Germany
and Communist
East Germany

Carolyn Gammon
Christiane Hemker

Translated from the German by
Carolyn Gammon

Wilfrid Laurier University Press
[WLU]

We acknowledge the support of the Canada Council for the Arts for our publishing program. We acknowledge the financial support of the Government of Canada through the Book Publishing Industry Development Program for our publishing activities.

Library and Archives Canada Cataloguing in Publication

Krause, Johanna, 1907–2001.
    Johanna Krause twice persecuted : surviving in Nazi Germany and Communist East Germany / Carolyn Gammon, Christiane Hemker.

(Life writing series)

Originally published Berlin : Metropol, c2004 under title: Zweimal verfolgt. Collaboration between Johanna Krause, Carolyn Gammon and Christiane Hemker. Translation by Carolyn Gammon.

ISBN 978-1-55458-006-4

    1. Krause, Johanna, 1907–2001. 2. Holocaust, Jewish (1939–1945)—Germany—Dresden—Personal narratives. 3. Women prisoners—Germany—Biography.
4. Ravensbrück (Concentration camp)—Biography. 5. Women—Germany (East)—Biography. 6. Dresden (Germany)—Biography. 7. Germany (East)—Biography.
I. Gammon, Carolyn, 1959– II. Hemker, Christiane III. Title. IV. Series.

DS134.42.K73A3 2007   940.53'18092   C2007-901769-X

Published by Wilfrid Laurier University Press
Waterloo, Ontario, Canada
www.wlupress.wlu.ca

For Johanna

In her youth, Johanna Krause was greatly supported by Dresden's Jewish community. In Johanna's name, therefore, royalties earned by this book will be donated to the Dresden Jewish community for work with children and youth.

All my life, I fought and fought and fought again. It's been decades that I've been fighting the Nazis. Actually, all I've done is fight fascism. And to think I'm just a small, unimportant woman.

That's just the way it is.

Contents

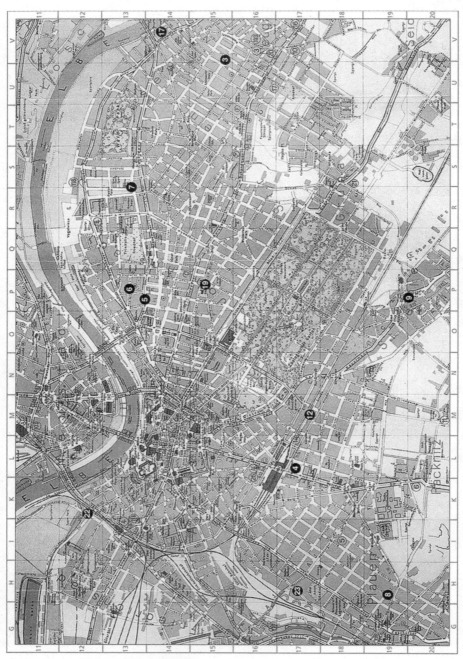

Dresden: overview. See legend, page x.

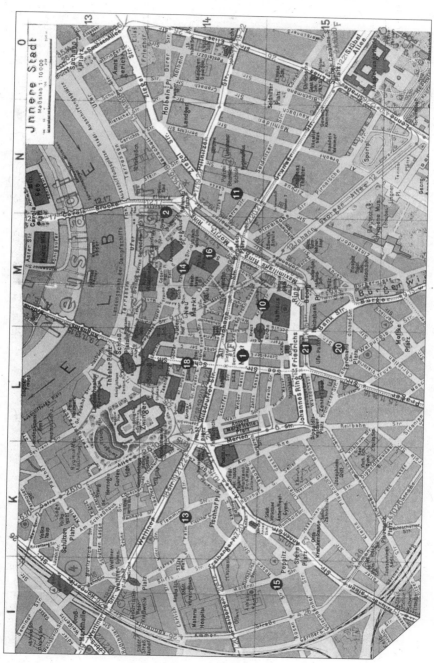

Dresden: the inner city. See legend, page x.

Dresden maps legend

Introduction
*by Freya Klier**

There are biographies that embrace an entire century. Johanna Krause's is such a biography. This small woman from Dresden lived in the time of the German Empire, the Weimar Republic, the Nazi period, forty years of East German communism, and then the unified Germany.

There are human fates that make your breath catch in your throat. Johanna Krause's is such a fate. She lived and suffered through two dictatorships. Two dictatorships: that means imprisonment for "insulting the Führer"; imprisonment for "defiling the race"; concentration camps, including Ravensbrück; and, after all that, imprisonment for "acts against the state" in East Germany.

While interviewing Johanna for our project of making a documentary film of her life, I often asked myself, how does a person stand all that? One answer I found is that the person must be protected by a bevy of angels.

And that is true of Johanna. For example, in the spring of 1945 when the SS drove more than one thousand women and girls on a death march through the Egerland in the Czech countryside, there were only three survivors. The Jewish woman from Dresden—Johanna—was one of them. She was a victim of typhoid, dysentery, starvation, and a severe blow to the head delivered by the rifle butt of an SS man. That she survived was a miracle.

---

* Freya Klier is a civil-rights activist, author, and filmmaker. Originally from Dresden, she was expelled from East Germany in 1988. In 1996, she made a documentary film about Johanna Krause entitled *Johanna: Eine Dresdner Ballade* (*Johanna: A Dresden Ballad*).

I

Portrait of Johanna Krause
by Christoph Wetzel. (Ravensbrück Concentration Camp
Memorial Museum.)

How does a person live through all that?

The next answer I found: perhaps if the person is supported by an extraordinary love story, as was the case with Johanna and her husband,
Max, an artist who was waiting at the prison door on the day she was released.

"My life was a never-ending roller coaster," this small woman from
Dresden said toward the end of her life. Yet her voice was full of astonish-
ment.

Johanna was the oldest person I had the pleasure of being friends with.
At the age of ninety-three, her back making a rainbow to earth, she died.

She was the opposite of a cuddly grandmother. Even in her diminish-
ing body there was such a fervent Hungarian temperament that she found
peace only with her last breath.

Like all those who live close to a century, Johanna suffered from lone-
liness. She survived her husband and long-time friends by many decades.
As a Jew living in the "wrong place" at the "wrong time," she was not al-

lowed to have children. In 1943, after German doctors cut a seven-and-a-half-month-old fetus out of her body, the nurse told her it was a boy. Johanna was young and still might have many children, she said. She meant well, but did she not know that the Jewish woman had been sterilized? "After the war," Johanna said, "my husband gave me two small puppies."

My encounter with Johanna, this vital and courageous woman, was for me a gift. I learned a lot from her about sincerity, bravery, and loyalty to one's friends. What hit her the hardest? The lies told by many of her contemporaries—a certain opportunism that, if necessary, rolled over dead bodies.

I hope this book is widely read because Johanna's courage and human decency can serve as a compass for future generations.

Carolyn Gammon and Christiane Hemker recorded Johanna's turbulent life story before it disappeared into the shadow of history like so many of the other stories we could have learned from. For their commitment and meticulous work, they have earned my utmost respect.

1 My Home

I was a child of the back streets. That's why I could master my life. My childhood allowed me to come to grips with my life. In my childhood I had no warm hearth, no love. I survived that. I was hungry and I survived that. At such a young age, I had already suffered so much that I could survive everything that came afterwards.

My mother belonged to the Jewish community. Her father was orthodox. She was born Johanna Lindner on January 23, 1874. The Lindners had a little house in Szenitz, Hungary, and a haulage business with horse and cart. Because of her father's business, my mother was always around horses. By the age of three or four, she was on horseback. This would later be her undoing.

I never knew my mother's brothers or sisters.

Her marriage followed Jewish orthodox tradition whereby the parents check out how much the man is worth and you wouldn't be asked if you love him. My grandfather chose my mother's future husband. That was not easy for her, but it was in keeping with Jewish tradition.

Her first husband was a Jew; he was a printer named Pollack. For the wedding he gave her a long gold chain like the women used to wear and a little purse in which to carry the chain and other beautiful jewellery. The young newlyweds lived in the same small town as my grandparents. In 1905, just two years after they married, my mother's husband died of lead poisoning, which was typical for people in that trade (hygienic standards were not what they are today). The couple had been childless, and my mother was a young widow. After her husband's death, many of his relatives tried to get this or that thing back from her. They said that certain things not been promised to her or were not rightfully hers after only two years of marriage. So my mother packed a small suitcase and went to Germany. The wedding jewellery she took with her, and it was enough, more than enough. My mother was a homey, countrified type. Where she found the courage to leave Hungary is a mystery. No one thought she would do it. She couldn't speak a word of German. German was taught in Hungarian schools, but she wouldn't have known more than "*Guten Tag.*"

My mother arrived in Dresden in 1905, and right away she joined the Hungarian association (there were Russian and English associations as well). She also went right away to the Jewish community, which found her both work and a room in Schössergasse 1 at the old marketplace.

In the years that followed, my mother earned a living from sewing, a trade she had learned in Hungary. She had a talent for sewing. Her specialty was decorative edging or trimming on jackets and blouses, lacework, tassels, and tufts. That was in high fashion. In fact, workers like her were in demand so she did this type of work in a factory.

Now, my mother heard that in Dresden-Reick there was horse racing. My mother had known horses since childhood. For her, horses were like children. So she went regularly to the horse racing and lost all her money betting.

My mother was a good-looking woman. Soon enough, she attracted the attention of a man at the racetrack. Clemens Oskar Hähnel was an elegant, charming, and attractive man with a good income. A commercial traveller at the time, he owned a huge piece of land with a villa in Pausitz bei Wurzen. Later he became director and then head of the firm where he worked. My mother saw him as a good match. She also believed, as many foreigners do, that he would help her obtain German citizenship.

For my mother, Hähnel was the first big love of her life. Their love affair lasted several months. Hähnel gave her his address, and he often came to Dresden on business. My mother trusted him. And then one day she was pregnant. She wrote to Hähnel immediately. The visits stopped. He had everything done through a lawyer and the court dealt with guardianship. My mother received a one-time payment of three thousand marks. There would be no more financial support. Hähnel had a lot of property, but he also had tax debts. He was a lady's man who lived beyond his means. But he didn't deny anything, because in the end my mother was a decent woman. It turned out that Hähnel was married and had two children; his wife lived in Pohl bei Leipzig. My mother had known nothing of that.

Some months later, after all the financial arrangements had been made with Mr. Hähnel, I was born out of wedlock to Johanna, born Lindner, widowed Pollack.

My mother recounted the whole story long after I was grown up. In fact, she did not tell me personally but spoke to my future husband instead. He wanted to marry me, and he asked her who my father was. At first she didn't want to tell him anything but then, under pressure, she told all. My father, Clemens Oskar Hähnel, had been born in Nieder-Langenau on May 17, 1876, and he was not Jewish. Throughout my childhood, I knew nothing about my father. I only had the feeling that the man my mother later married was not my father.

On October 23, 1907, I was born Johanna Lindner in Dresden's Imperial and Royal Women's Hospital. Because what little money my mother had was lost at the races, and because she had no access to the state money for my care, she gave me to a foster mother right after my birth. This woman took my story to heart and tried to adopt me. But then she got very ill and died. I spent the next four years in the care of another woman arranged for by the officials. In 1913, after six years in foster care, my mother took me back. In that entire time, she had not visited me once. She remained tight-lipped about it and for the longest time I knew nothing. Now I only know that my second foster mother didn't want to give me back and mourned losing me.

Why did my mother take me back? She was involved with another man and wanted to become a real German wife. His name was Karl Samel and he was a master tailor. He was not Jewish. His family was from Goldert in Prussia, but I think they were related somehow to the circus Samels in Dresden. He had a sister in Dresden and a brother in Berlin who was a tailor as well. The most intellectually deficient of the entire family was the Samel my mother married. He was a big nothing who didn't want my mother to take me back. But he couldn't have any children, and so after the wedding in 1913 he adopted me. The adoption was later annulled by the Nazis.

We moved into an apartment in Kreuzstrasse 11. In the same building was a bar named the Katacomben. The owners of this bar sold skulls and all sorts of junk. Our apartment had a spacious hallway, a huge sewing room, a big kitchen, and a large room that doubled as a living room and bedroom. There were, of course, petroleum lamps and outdoor toilets. But there were no radios yet, and no electricity or gas. All that came later.

I was so naïve. I put out bits of sugar because I thought that the stork would come and bring me a brother or a sister. I wanted siblings because Samel was not good to me. He beat me and later, when I was a teenager, tormented me too. But that's getting ahead of my story.

In 1914, the First World War broke out and Samel was drafted. They had to take every man because military technology was not sophisticated back then; it was hand-to-hand combat with guns. Even those who couldn't become soldiers were taken from their trades as shoemakers or tailors or gardeners and put to work in the military barracks. This period was tolerable for me because Samel was out of the picture. On occasion, he would visit us (still in his uniform), but that wasn't too bad.

I was registered with the Jewish congregation. Because we were so poor, I was allowed to go to the Jewish summer camp in Ober-Rochwitz. For me it was a wonderland; there were swings and Lea the nurse with her white cap. We wore wooden shoes. The poor kids all had lice. Because I had naturally curly hair, Lea deloused me right away. Then the counsellors made little caps for all of us. I was there three or four weeks in the summer holidays, and those were the best times of my childhood.

I made it to the eighth grade. At that time, there was a district school, a civic school, and (for people with money) a high school. We had no money, so I started at the district school. Later, with the aid of the Jewish community, I attended the civic school. But I did not learn much there either. The two schools were beside one another on Georgeplatz.

The teachers used to punish us for every little thing. They would beat us with sticks. During the war, there were no men around. We had a female teacher, a real dragon, who almost always had the stick in her hands. She would beat you if you were a couple of minutes late, if your stomach growled in hunger, or even if your feet had frozen in your wooden shoes and you groaned a bit.

One time I took a liberty. There were coaches in those days, and once I pulled myself up onto the back of one without paying. The coach driver chased me off with his whip, and I lost my satchel. So I ended up at school

Ferienheim Ober-Rochwitz

die „Lunge" unserer Großstadtjugend

The Jewish summer camp in Ober-Rochwitz that Johanna attended as a child. (*Dresdner Hefte* 29, no. 12 [1994]: 65.)

without my satchel and got beaten on my frozen hands. That was the time I lived in. That's why I call myself a child of the back streets.

We learned handiwork and especially knitting. It was wartime and so we knitted socks for the soldiers, a skill that came in handy years later. During religious instruction, I had to leave because I was Jewish. I was allowed to hang around the school until it was over. I was pretty lonely. There was another Jewish girl in my class. She lived at Altmarkt, the old marketplace, and her parents owned a restaurant. That helped me a lot. In my other class, there was a Jewish girl who came from the Weinberg family, which had many daughters. Her father was a shoemaker.

I was friends with the girl whose parents had a restaurant at Altmarkt called Roth's Restaurant. This Roth girl was smaller than I and I was already among the smallest in the class, but at least she had enough to eat at the restaurant. She had a nanny, too, because her parents were working and unable to look after the children, and another woman who ran the house; I knew nothing of this type of lifestyle. There was also a female tutor. Our teacher was often sick and so school would be cancelled. There were no substitute teachers in those days because all the men were at war. At the Roth's house, I participated in the tutoring. And I could eat! My school friend sometimes gave me leftovers to take home to my mother.

There was another girl I befriended for practical reasons. Her parents had a fish shop at Gerokstrasse 61. The mother's name was Gertrud Suchy and her shop was called Suchy's. Years later, when I was a young woman, I went to that house on Gerokstrasse to pay my rent for a new print shop. "You know, you have a unique face," the landlady said. "You seem so familiar." She called for her daughter (now named Gertrud Herzog), and the daughter said, "But that's Hanna. We went to school together."

At first I didn't recognize her. That's how life is sometimes. You don't recognize someone even though you were friends as children.

As the daughter of a fish merchant, Gertrud was lonely: she smelled of fish. There was nothing she could do about it; her whole body smelled of fish and the other children didn't want to sit beside her. I made friends with her despite the smell because I was invited to eat at her house and sometimes I could take food home to my mother. Her family was well off.

I didn't have any of that childhood stuff like birthday parties, except when my friends had one. Birthday parties at the Roth's were a great pleasure. At other people's homes, I had a chance to eat cake. That was what I experienced as "mother love." I didn't get that at home.

I was clever. I had to be clever because I was always hungry, and at home there was only rutabaga, rutabaga, and again rutabaga. There was rarely anything sweet. There were Sahnesara candies that were made by a well-known company, but you had to stand in line to get them. At that time, Dresden was awash in bedbugs; they crawled up into your clothes as you stood in line. I always cried when my mother told me that we had to stand in line. She would line up first and then I would replace her, and every time I brought bedbugs home with me. Dresden rid itself of bedbugs only after the Allied bombing during World War II.

Much of the time we had nothing to eat. When the money was gone and there was nothing on the table (because my mother had lost her money on the horses yet again), she would say to me: "Go to the city hall where the golden donkey is and where the hackney carriages come in. Do a little curtsy and then open the door of the carriage. When the ladies step out with their long coats and ostrich feather hats, say to them: 'Allow me, madam, please watch your step' or 'Madam, may I be of assistance?' Then pick up their long skirts with the braid trimming and curtsy again. When you have enough money for bread, move on to the next one." All this time she was making me two little braids, left and right, with ribbons.

At the city hall, I competed with poor boys who were also hanging out at the carriages. We were like a clique. There were many boys and just two girls, and sometimes we beat each other up. I was a scrappy little thing, so I never left before I had enough money for bread. Then I would go home and give my mother the money. But first I would say to her, "I want a whole bag of cake crusts." You could get such a bag for five or ten cents at the bakery, and I wouldn't give my mother any of it. I had earned those cake crusts and she could eat the bread. It's because of stories like this that I say I was child of the back streets. I had to earn money for bread because my mother lost most of our money betting, and Samel was away at war. I can understand why my mother spent her money at the racetrack; she grew up with horses after all. I don't gamble myself—won't touch anything like that.

The Jewish community supported me. We were a big community with poor people and rich people. The Jewish department stores gave away clothes that had been displayed in showcase windows and were a bit bleached by the sun. That's why I had outfits from Goldmann's or Alsberg's; I could never have afforded them myself. And I wasn't the only one. There were many poor Jews. People dropped items off at the synagogue, and the community sorted and distributed them.

In the synagogue, the rich Jews had reserved seats that had to be paid for. We paid nothing and so we stood. It didn't matter to us. I was a small, thin thing and more often than not someone would say to me, "Come and sit beside me or sit on my lap."

In the meanwhile, at the district school I stuck to the Roth girl and the girl whose parents had a fish shop. Later I got to know Lea Langer, who was two years older than me. Her father, Moses Langer, ran a furniture and clothing business that covered a whole floor on Brüdergasse. Lea's future husband, the painter Hans Grundig, was well known in Dresden. I bought some of his paintings.

Thanks to the sponsorship of the Jewish community, I was able to switch from the district school to the civic school. But first we moved and I started attending the elementary school on Silbermannstrasse. Because of the move, I saw less of the Roth girl and Gertrud from the fish shop. We lived at Stephanienplatz 4, a large six-story house that doesn't exist anymore. After we moved, when I was about thirteen, I started learning Hebrew with Dr. Eva Stein. She ran something like a service for the poor and

The Old Synagogue of Dresden, circa 1870. (Saxon State and University Library Dresden, German Photothek #181772.)

she looked after us. She was a member of the Jewish community and she became my religious instructor. That particular year, Hebrew lessons didn't take place in the community offices; we met instead at Sachsenplatz.

My mother was deeply religious. She could speak Hebrew backwards and forwards, and she took me to the synagogue when I was just a tiny child. But when it came to Hebrew, I was extremely lazy. Why is that? In Kreuzstrasse, we had the one large room with two beds in one direction and the other at right angles. We all slept in the same room, and I slept in the bed at the back. My stepfather slept on the other side. My mother had a peculiar habit. She talked in her sleep, and not in German but in Hungarian and Hebrew. I couldn't get to sleep. Hungarian is a chatterbox language, and I rejected Hebrew because my mother spoke it incessantly in her sleep the whole night long! She could recite the prayer books from cover to cover.

As well as our apartment in the city, my family—although I don't call them my family anymore because I had a very bad childhood—rented two walk-in lockers in Bilzbad. On Saturdays, my mother would go to Bilzbad

The elementary school on Silbermannstrasse, circa 1938. (Saxon State and University Library Dresden, German Photothek #58479. Photo by Walter Moebius.)

and spend the night there. I really wanted to go with her, but she never let me. One day my stepfather molested me and nearly beat me to death. A neighbour, a woman in the house at Stephanienplatz, realized at some point that something was going on. Samel had done this to me many times, and I screamed because he hurt me so much. My stepfather did not like me. And dumb as I was, I didn't know that he wasn't allowed to beat me. I was fifteen or sixteen years old at the time.

Anyway, the neighbour called the police. They sent Mrs. Mai to evaluate the situation. Mrs. Mai owned a bookstore on Marschnerstrasse. She was not Jewish. She did volunteer welfare work for the church, and I was one of the youth she looked after so we didn't go to the dogs. Mrs. Mai decided that I had to leave that house. So I moved out, and thanks to my religious instructor, Dr. Stein, I was given a small room at Rosenstrasse 43. The Salvation Army occupied the back house and they were always singing in the courtyard.

I moved in with a single woman who had cancer. One of her breasts had been removed. She was very happy to have someone there to help take care of her. I had a tiny room with a bed, a folding chair, a petroleum

Dr. Jakob Winter, Johanna's legal
guardian. (*Die Juden in Sachsen, ihr Leben
und Leiden* [Leipzig: Gesellschaft für
Christlich-Jüdische Zusammenarbeit
Dresden e.V.], p. 24.)

lamp, and a radio. Mrs. Mai gave me sheets for the bed. The room cost five
marks fifty. The radio, which came with headphones, cost an extra fifty
cents a month. That was when the first radios came out and you had to use
headphones.

I needed a new guardian because the guardianship was taken away
from Samel. He had nothing more to say in my life. When my mother remained with him, I was deeply hurt. But what could I do? Some things in
this world are beyond comprehension.

Some people have a happy childhood, and others don't. You can't choose
your parents. I know though that my mother was not satisfied with herself or her past. She had no contact with her own family in Hungary and
she never told me anything about her past. She kept everything secret.

I don't like to talk about this time of my life.

Then I had the biggest stroke of luck. Dr. Stein took on my cause and
arranged for Dr. Jakob Winter, the chief rabbi of Dresden, to become my
new guardian. A square in Dresden-Prohlis is named after Dr. Winter. I had
already known him for a long time. He was good to me. When I was a
child, he gave me a doll carriage and a big Käthe Kruse doll. Receiving
gifts was something new for me. Out of sheer envy, other children wrecked
my doll, and it was partly my fault because I had gone around bragging
about it. That's how kids are.

Over the years, I had talked myself into believing that Dr. Winter was my real father. He had many wards beside myself, but I gave him the hardest time. Whenever he tried to take me home, I would pitch a fit. I didn't want to go. Once I even bit him in the leg. I asked him why I couldn't stay with him like you would stay with your father—for I saw him as my father. I had a wild character. I was high-spirited, curious, and hungry for life. I got on his nerves with my constant questions: What's that and where's that? He was so patient, but I sure didn't make it easy for him.

When I became somewhat more independent later on, I started visiting him myself. We would go places together or he would lend me books. Of course, he taught me all sorts of things having to do with religious instruction and general education. "You shouldn't do that," he would say. "It is not correct." I loved having him to myself. I couldn't stand it if other children were around. How can I put it? I was a child who needed love. I always wanted to cuddle with him because I received no love at home. Not from my mother either. Rabbi Winter was a wonderful man because he understood me so well. He gave me something that stayed with me my entire life.

A rabbi must be wise. He must have an unblemished past. He must be educated in music. He must be a psychologist and embody all the good qualities. Dr. Jakob Winter was all that. A chief rabbi today is very different.

After I left home, Dr. Stein looked after me much of the time. I was alone, still a youth (you came of age at twenty-one in those days). The rabbi, Dr. Stein, and the community took care of me. They gave me extra allowances and subscriptions for food. These were given to students to help them out but also to poor Jews. Sister Lea, the nurse, cooked for me. On holidays she brought me challah and fruit. She knew that I needed it. Now that I'm old and could really use a nurse it would be a dream come true if our Jewish community would organize something like this. But it doesn't work that way.

Once my school years were behind me, and I didn't fail a class (not that I learned much), Dr. Stein arranged for me to interview for a position as an apprentice. Apprenticeships were scarce, but Dr. Stein had connections. On Waisenhausstrasse was the fashion house Johanna Hunger run by this very tall, distinguished lady. It resembled the stylish boutiques of today. Mrs. Hunger was a Christian who had an affinity with Jews. So

Dr. Stein asked her if I could get a position as a milliner's apprentice in a studio at Münchner Platz.

As it happens, I ended up training to be a saleswoman. I was too wild and restless. I couldn't sit still, so after just two weeks Mrs. Hunger came to me and said, "Listen Hanna, I can't use you as a milliner. You have hot pepper in your blood."

"Yes," I said, "my mother is Hungarian after all." Then I started to cry because I thought I was losing my position as a trainee. But she replied, "You don't need to cry. I'm going to make a fantastic saleswoman out of you."

There were two of us who learned to be saleswomen in the business on Waisenhausstrasse. The other girl was not Jewish. Sometimes she cried because I found it so easy to persuade the customers to make a purchase. When we lived on Kreuzstrasse, I had sold Pflaumentöffelchen (plum sweets), little figures fashioned out of dried plums skewered on sticks to resemble chimney sweeps. Every Sunday at the Altmarkt, when there was a small orchestra playing, I would sit in a little folding chair with wooden legs and cloth in the middle. Gentlemen strolled through the marketplace with their top hats and silver walking sticks, and the ladies wore long dresses with velvet trimming and ostrich feathers. They promenaded, sneaking little looks and winking at each other. Some of these encounters led to marriages or love affairs. During all of this, I sold my plum chimney sweeps. You could buy them in bulk and pay for them later. My mother organized everything. I only had to sell. And you can imagine when a cute little thing says to you, "Plum sweets, would you like some plum sweets?" People loved to buy from me. I did that after school or especially when there was no school.

Some years later, I sold shoes at the Renner department store on Altmarkt, but it wasn't my forte. I had worked in a fashion house and had developed quite a different style with the ladies. I acquired very good manners. I had already learned from my guardian, the chief rabbi, to address the women as "madam." I already knew how to hold a conversation with well-educated people. "You have such a lovely tall figure," I would say. "I would suggest a batiste hat with small roses. That would suit you beautifully. Oh, you look splendid in it!"

For women who were shorter I would recommend other hats. I was friendly and nice, and I chatted with the customers. From the moment

The Renner department store at Dresden's old marketplace, 1934. (Saxon State University Library Dresen, German Photothek #M5020. Photo by Walter Moebius.)

they walked in the door, I looked after their needs and therefore I made good sales. I was Mrs. Hunger's best saleswoman. Her customers came from around the world. Sometimes, as a young trainee, I delivered large hat boxes to the Weigler Sanatorium (one of the two sanatoriums in Weissen Hirsch, Dresden). In the foyer, I would not let myself be put off by the doorman.

"I would like to bring madam her hat personally."

When I arrived at madam's quarters, of course, I made a big ceremony out of it. I could talk up a storm.

"Take your time, madam. And here is the bill. I would be very grateful if you could pay me now and let me give you a receipt right away."

I would get a tip—and I needed it. That was the most important thing. That's why I went right upstairs instead of leaving the hat with the doorman. Those were the days.

2 After My Apprenticeship

I had finished my training to be a saleswoman. I was eighteen years old and lived alone in my little room at Rosenstrasse 43 with the woman who had cancer. I had no money and had to look for work. It was a rough time. The after-effects of World War I could still be felt. If you were unemployed, you had to take whatever work they offered you. You couldn't say, "I won't do that." If they sent you off to work as a dishwasher in a house on Altmarkt, you had to go.

"Please don't give me just washing jobs," I told my unemployment officer. "I live in a tiny room with a woman who has cancer. Please give me something else the moment you have it."

There were a few workers at the unemployment office who investigated where you had already worked and if you were good and honest. If you approached them a second time and you had not been good at your work, you wouldn't be taken on again.

In 1925, I ended up at Koch & Sterzel, a large optical instrument business. I was there for two years, and I earned twelve marks a week. At first I worked in the painting section, but then I got the nickel itch. Mr. Miertsch, who became my supervisor, said, "The little one should come to me for lacquer work because she has the nickel sickness." So I did lacquer work on the optical and measuring instruments. Mr. Miertsch often brought me a couple of sandwiches. I would probably have starved without them. From the twelve marks, I had to pay 5.50 for the little room. I also had to pay for the petroleum (there were no electric lights back then), and there was the fifty cents for the radio. My money just didn't hold out.

The Jewish community continued to provide me with clothing and sheets because I couldn't afford to buy anything myself. I wore the clothes supplied by Goldmann's and other Jewish stores, and I always looked good. I knew how to deck myself out. You couldn't tell that I was a poor girl when I was out on the street. I was happy to have a little room and a job.

Sometimes I was a bit sloppy at work because I loved to read so much. The supervisor would bring me newspapers and other things to read, but when the bell rang and the break was over, you had to get back to work. One time the boss caught me reading after the break. For that, one mark was deducted from my salary, so I was down to eleven marks a week. But the supervisor helped me out; he had children himself after all.

After the lacquer work, I was transferred to the big mechanics room and a new supervisor, Master Rabe. The room was full of mechanics. I sat behind the supervisor and did the calculations for the piecework. I did not feel very comfortable there. When taking piecework to the supervisor, I had to walk by the mechanics and they brayed like donkeys. It was just like running the gauntlet, and it made me sick.

I left Koch & Sterzel and went to the cigarette factory. I had already worked there during the Christmas holidays in 1927 and then for two months in the summer of 1928. In 1927, I worked in the Greiling cigarette factory in the Yenidze, an impressive building in Dresden that looks like a mosque from the outside. The factory produced Attika cigarettes and better-quality cigarettes that were decorated with a golden brass band or a small bow. I earned forty-five marks a week (not even the mechanics at Koch & Strezel earned that much)—money I could use to pay off all my debts. But then one day when I left the factory a group of women who worked in the Yenidze were standing outside, and they threatened to beat me up. "Piecework kills!" they yelled, because I had worked so fast and earned so much money. An inspector called Götze had watched me work and he had told me that I was doing really well with the piecework, and that I was a fast worker. But it hurt my colleagues because they were told, "If Johanna can get so much piecework done today, you can too."

Of course, money was at the root of it all. The women didn't know that I was poor because I was always so nicely dressed. Also, I was a bit snobbish and I enjoyed the fact that they were all looking at me. But like any young girl, I didn't think all those things through. The women never understood that I was really struggling.

Women rolling cigarettes in the Yendize cigarette factory, before 1945. (Saxon State and University Library Dresden, German Photothek #46454.)

When the women threatened to beat me up, the men came and protected me. One of them even wanted to marry me. He had been a blacksmith at Koch & Sterzel, and now he worked as a mechanic at the cigarette factory. He was a big, handsome man and would have made an excellent catch. He came from a good home and was above reproach. But I wasn't interested. I was still running after life and all its experiences. He was a solid fellow but too calm and even-tempered for me. Still, he was a good friend at the time. We went out together after work sometimes but then went our separate ways. It was the kind of friendship where you meet again years later and tell each other what you've been up to.

I told him about my family troubles and that I had to be careful because my stepfather often stalked me. In fact, one time my friend even experienced this with me. This fellow had given me a beautiful lacquered purse for my birthday. It was the first valuable gift that I'd ever received. My friend had worked hard to pay for that purse. One day we were walking down the street and my stepfather approached us. He took the purse away from me, tore it up, and stomped on it until it was destroyed. My stepfather was always hunting me down like a bloodhound even though he was officially forbidden to do so. He followed me everywhere. When he noticed that I was alone and couldn't protect myself, he would thrash me. It's impossible to imagine such a thing if you haven't gone through something like it yourself.

At some point, the golden ribbons from the cigarettes started to give me a rash on my hands. Big blisters formed, and I couldn't do this work anymore. But I had saved a lot of money. I spent only thirty cents on food and saved the rest. During that Christmas season when I had first started working at the cigarette factory, I went twice a week to a little restaurant on Ammonstrasse to eat a hot meal. It was in this restaurant that I met a young man named Max Eisenhardt. He had watched me awhile, how I came to the restaurant twice a week and ate two dumplings in sauce, nothing more. That cost thirty cents at the time. He asked himself why someone who looked so snazzy would just eat dumplings and not order anything to drink. At some point, he approached me and invited me for a meal. He paid for the drinks too. I had always been alone there after all.

Max Eisenhardt earned a good living from setting the type in a big print shop, but then he'd blow the money. One day he invited me to his place. I can still remember his room. There was a large gramophone from France and French records (chansons and such) belonging to his landlady.

Eisenhardt was a screwball and a show-off. A sign on his door read: "Immograph Max Eisenhardt." I was ready to leave when I saw that. I thought to myself, you don't want to have anything to do with an "immograph." He noticed that I wanted to go and coaxed me back upstairs. I asked him what an immograph was, and he said that he was a graphologist—he interpreted handwriting—and a printer.

At some point, Max Eisenhardt suggested that we open our own print shop. After thinking about it for a bit, I looked for space to rent in the house with the fish shop at Gerokstrasse 61; it cost thirty-five marks a month. We also leased a high-speed printing machine. I paid for the hand press and all the other necessities. We printed business cards and *Spartacus*, one of the early communist papers. We called our business the Dresden Book and Art Print Shop. It ran under my name because a couple of years before Max Eisenhardt had to make a financial oath of disclosure and so could no longer run a business on his own. I did it because he was my friend. It was only later on that I realized he was a nutcase. Being a young woman, I couldn't read his character at first.

Johanna in the 1930s. (Estate of Johanna Krause.)

So, we opened the print shop in 1930. Over the next three years, despite all the hard work and drudgery it took to run that shop, I never saw a cent. During the day I worked at Yenidze, and then in the evenings I stood at the hand press while Max worked the high-speed press. I didn't trust myself to work the high-speed press; Max, on the other hand, had experience.

One day on my way to work I stopped by the famous Bear's Bar on Webergasse for a coffee and a piece of cake. There was a man sitting at my table, and we struck up a conversation. He told me that he was a printer with a shop of his own.

"I have a print shop too," I said. "But I've never made a cent from it."

"My business is going well," he replied. "I'll give you a couple of our contracts."

The man didn't want to take up with me or anything; he was married. The contacts he gave me just emerged from our conversation. But I never benefited from those contacts because Eisenhardt printed them and kept the proceeds for himself. He didn't give me any money at all.

Spartacus didn't bring in any money either. The papers were ordered and picked up. The person picking them up signed the invoice under a false name. No one signing for those papers ever used a real name. We didn't know this at first. When fascism began, we didn't see a cent from printing Spartacus.

I used up all my savings on the print shop. Max Eisenhardt, who didn't work much, squandered all the money. By that point, we had nothing more than a business partnership. He carried on with other women, and I ended up paying them when they helped us with the printing. Eisenhardt was cunning. He had many children with these women but never paid any support. He always found willing victims. When I was imprisoned in 1933 for "insulting the Führer" and couldn't return to the print shop, I signed over everything to Eisenhardt.

Getting to know artists interested me a lot more than all that nonsense at the print shop or the cigarette factory. My dreams were those of another world ... they were my dreams. As a child I would lie in bed at night and think to myself, as the lights flickered, this is not how you want your life to be. I was like a game, a game of marbles. I wanted to see and experience so much. And so it came to be, with my guardian angel always by my side.

One thing was paramount: I never wanted to have anything to do with people who were small-minded. I was always searching for something greater. Most important, the man I loved would have to be a very good man.

3 Dancing Was My Life

I wanted to be a dancer. That was my dream. When I was in school at Stephanienplatz, I had friends who were in ballet. One day I went to the big ballet school on Ostbahnstrasse. The school was run by Gret Palucca. She lived on my street and I knew her personally.

"I really want to become a dancer." I said to her. "But first I have to perform something for you."

And I danced for her. I danced for my life.

"You move well," she told me. "You have élan and charm. But I really can't take you on. You're too short."

I was barely five feet tall. It would have been difficult financially as well. No one had anything to give away. Gret Palucca was a communist, but her communism ended when it came to money. That's when I started my apprenticeship. Still, dancing was my life. Up until a few years ago, I still danced the night away at the *Volkssolidarität*, the People's Solidarity Association parties. And all my female friends were ballet dancers.

In 1933, something terrible—involving a ballet dancer—happened to me. At that time, people hung out at bars because they didn't have the time or money for parties. If you wanted to go dancing, you would stand in front of an establishment and stare at the doorman.

"What's up?" he would eventually ask. "You want in?"

"No money," you would reply.

You would stand there for a good half hour, until finally he said, "Come on, get in there!"

And so you danced the whole evening. You had no money to buy a drink, but you danced and were happy that you looked good and could dance well.

An der Ostbahnstraße (On Ostbahn Street), painting by Otto Griebel, circa 1930. (Otto Griebel, *Ich war ein Mann der Strasse. Lebenserinnerungen eines Dresdner Malers (I Was a Man of the Streets: The Memoirs of a Dresden Painter)* [Dresden 1986, 2nd printing 1995], p. 157.)

There were bars like Café Zuntz on Prager Strasse where Otto Griebel, Otto Dix, and other artists hung out. I went there too. None of us—not even someone like Dix—had money. I wasn't interested in money then; only later did it interest me. But the world of artists ... now that was my world.

Big business people would come to the bar and talk with the artists because they valued their world and found them fascinating. Sometimes they paid for our drinks. The artists told one another amazing stories about their artwork and their lives. It was completely informal. No one cared if you had a hole in your stocking or if your heel was uneven. In the world of artists, such things were of no concern. And *that* was my world.

It was in this artists' place that I got to know the ballerina. She sometimes had coffee there. It was friendship at first sight. Her name was Ulrike, but I called her Uschi. She was from Dresden and attended the Palucca School. She came from a good home. We became friends.

"Do you know what we should do?" she said to me one day. "We should go to the cabaret at Café Altmarkt."

That's how all my suffering began.

We emptied our purses. Uschi received a modest allowance from home and had yet to earn a living as a ballerina. Neither of us had any money to speak of. At that time, you received twelve marks a week if you were unemployed; after that you had to fend for yourself. Uschi and I had learned knitting and crocheting at school and so we made ourselves beautiful, colourful bags. To avoid paying the coat check at Café Altmark, we put our coats in these bags.

Uschi drank lemonade and—I was already drinking alcohol by that time—I had a glass of beer. That's all we could afford. We were such dumb young girls. I had borrowed a dress and high heels. I'd never worn high heels before, so I walked around like a stork on stilts. Uschi's aunt had lent me the shoes.

"Watch out that nothing happens to those shoes," Uschi had said as she handed them over.

"Of course," I said.

I had no idea what was coming my way.

There we were in Café Altmark, the two of us seated at a round table for four. We could see everything from there. It was the smallest table and stood right up at the front by the stage. On stage there were singers and dancers and other performers. How we laughed! Recently I was in a streetcar, and the sight of two young things laughing their heads off reminded me of how Uschi and I used to laugh at everything without even knowing what we were laughing about. Of course, we were much more naïve. We didn't know any of those things young people know nowadays. It would have been a sin for us to know such things. Thirteen-year-olds today are having children, God help us.

So we sat there sipping our drinks. I had my beer, Uschi her lemonade. My drinking beer upset her. "Some day I may forgive you for it," she told me. "Thank God you don't have enough money for a second one." Alcohol wasn't her thing. She lived in a different world, a ballerina's world. She wore hand-knitted stockings. I had knitted those wonderful stockings for her because I knew that a ballerina's legs are her most prized possession.

At some point, a tall, stately man approached our table and asked if one of the empty chairs was available. I looked at him and he looked good. He was five foot ten, had a super figure and big blue eyes. This is an honest man, I thought to myself. He could be an artist. And so I said to him, "Please be seated." Anything artistic drew me in. I had always told myself that if I married, I would marry an artist. Uschi looked sideways at me. I was always a bit more brazen, a bit more saucy than she was.

After some time, the show began. Suddenly a swarm of SA men burst into the café. There was about twenty of them. Fascism started with the SA; they were the precursors to the SS.

An SA man came to our table and wanted to drink my beer.

"I have no money, and that's my beer," I said. "It stays here."

"Can I sit here?" he asked.

"No, you can't. My colleague is in the lady's room, and it's her chair."

"You're lying," Uschi whispered to me.

"Yes, and I have my reasons," I replied. "I don't want anything to do with these people."

The SA men were all in uniform, all in uniform! You could see a Hitler in every one of them. I hated them and I still hate them to this day. I have hated fascists and narrow-minded people my whole life. These feelings developed in me unconsciously at a very young age, but when fascism came I felt it the most. It was in my blood. Where did it come from? It was their dreadful hatred of Jews. They wanted to exterminate Jews.

As we sat there, a flamenco dancer appeared on stage. You could see that he was Jewish. The SA could see it too because they stormed the stage, threw him off, and hit his head—*bang!*—against the stage wall. They stomped on him with their boots. I stood up, took off my borrowed high heels, and whacked an SA man over the head with them. They beat me black and blue and sent me flying down the staircase into a window. I was agile and defended myself as best I could.

The old marketplace was full of people because of the raid. We were to be taken to the police station on Schössergasse. The tall man who had sat at our table was still there. But Uschi was gone. "Johanna," she later explained, "my legs are my most valuable resource. I would lose my place at the ballet school and my mother would beat me if I had taken part in something like that."

We weren't even supposed to be at Café Altmarkt. We hadn't told anyone that we were going. We had just wanted to have the experience. The clothes and shoes belonging to Uschi's aunt were clearly no longer usable; the dress was ripped, the shoes ruined. And I was half naked as I stood there in the old marketplace.

Then I did the following. In my rage, I started to yell.

"You riffraff, you criminals! Your Hitler means war! Hitler is a murderer! You'll see soon enough, you scoundrels!"

I held nothing back, and the SA men beat me even more. I was the only one who defended the Jewish dancer. I don't know what became of him. It all happened just because he was Jewish and "Jew" meant something to the SA.

The brawl lasted a long time. It's a miracle I wasn't more seriously injured. Even though it seemed that the whole city had turned up at the old marketplace, no one but the tall man came to my assistance. At some point, they took us to the police station on Schössergasse and he came voluntarily as a witness. Later—much later—he became my husband.

He was an athlete and mountain climber, and he had done some boxing. On top of that, he was a skilled craftsman, an art metalworker, and had worked as an artist, a painter. He had brains too. As an athlete, he was tall with wide shoulders and so was able to protect me somewhat from the men who beat me during the brawl. "Man! Don't be so mean!" he had shouted at them as he tried to shield me from the blows.

For the longest time, we couldn't leave the police station because the SA were lying in wait for us outside. The SA were not arrested. They could do anything they wanted. We were sitting ducks. They finally took off at four in the morning, and we were released from the police station an hour later. The tall man accompanied me home.

"Well, I wonder what's going to happen now," he said as we parted. "You were swearing up a storm."

Sure enough, the police charged me with "insulting the Führer." *Insulting the Führer*. For God's sake!

I didn't deny it.

There was a court case. I was not only naïve but dumb to boot. I told the judge that the SA man had hit me. Of course I swore, but only because the man had beaten me so badly. The judge asked me what the man looked like. "I tore his cap off," I answered, "and, yes, I think—you don't have much hair yourself—he was about your size." The judge had to swallow his laughter.

I received a four-month sentence for insulting the Führer. I was lucky. It was right before the elections or I would have been a given much longer sentence. So, in 1933, I had my first conviction. I was put into the jail at Münchner Platz, which doesn't exist anymore.

In prison, I worked in the laundry room. I worked the presses. The four months didn't bother me. Prison food was better than anything I'd ever had on the outside. I didn't take my imprisonment seriously. At least I'd shown them that a small woman could defend herself! I didn't care. I was thick-skinned. I had no one in my life anyway.

Following the incident at Café Altmarkt, the Jewish community kept their distance. They didn't want me making a spectacle of myself. Most were timid and they retreated right away; later, many of them emigrated. They weren't like me. I was a crazy head from a working-class family. Not that I had anything in common with my mother. She was a peace-loving, religious person. I was unruly. I take after my father.

During my imprisonment, I withdrew from the community. I didn't deregister, but I lost touch with them.

On the day I was released, the tall man who had tried to protect me during the brawl was waiting for me at the prison door. His name was Max Krause.

"Oy! What are you doing here?" I asked, taken aback.

He said that he'd been in court during my case and knew I was being released today. "You're really one of a kind. The way you started pounding that guy with your heels! I could never forget you. I just wanted take you out for a drink to celebrate your release."

Now Max Eisenhardt was with one of his "flirts" and wasn't there. So Max Krause and I went to a little wine bar on Oberseegasse. Mother Anna, the bar's owner, was known all over Dresden. And the bar was full of artists. I had no tolerance for bourgeois people myself. I knew that artists had a different kind of lifestyle. I was a person who wanted to live freely and without the usual pressures, so the life of an artist meant something to me. They're more interesting, too. A circle of artists—that's where you find the intellects. It's in those circles you get that certain something.

So we were at this comfy but stylish place and, wouldn't you know it, bad luck hounded me again. First off, I was very shy. I felt out of place in the stylish wine bar. I didn't know anything about this kind of establishment. I had never in my life sat on a high bar stool. Max Krause asked me if I wanted a glass of wine and then started chatting with a scientist. At that point, I didn't know about patrons of the arts—people who understood the financial world and who talked to artists and offered them drinks. When the scientist asked me if I wanted something to drink, I said no thank you but he ordered me a glass of sparkling wine anyway.

I sat there sipping my sparkling wine as the two men talked. Suddenly a man sat down next to me. I ignored him at first, but then he put his arm around me and tried to feel me up. I looked at his face and immediately recognized Mr. Sollbrich, the policeman who had attacked me during the Café Altmarkt incident—the one I had used such choice words on. He was the Nazi pig who had testified against me during the hearing.

I turned to Max. "Look, it's Mr. Sollbrich. He's harassing me. Please help me off this bar stool."

Max nearly threw Sollbrich out of the place. I was in shock. That's it, I thought, you're going back to jail. I offered to leave the bar.

"Nothing more is going to happen," the owner assured me. "He's going to have to watch himself. I saw exactly what went on there—how he grabbed you. You don't have to be afraid. Max Krause is a really good person. Please stay."

So we stayed awhile. Sollbrich made himself scarce. Max wanted to go after him and beat him up, but I told him to let it be. Max then took me home. I cried the whole way. "I'm fresh out of jail and this happens. What if something comes of it?"

"Nothing's going to happen," Max consoled me. "I know Mother Anna. She'll deny that anything happened. You don't have to be afraid."

But I was afraid—although nothing came of it, thank God. Much later, one of Max's colleagues told me that Mr. Sollbrich was drafted and died in the war.

After that evening, Max Krause invited me and my friend Uschi out for coffee. Uschi always had to be so careful about what she ate. She couldn't afford to put on an ounce. But I sure ate! I even ate her food. I was terribly hungry.

It never occurred to me that my friendship with Max Krause might take a romantic turn. He was nearly six feet tall and powerfully built, whereas I was a small, thin mouse. At first I regarded him as a father figure. He was only five years older, but I looked much younger than I was; sometimes I even had to show my ID to get into a bar. Besides, Max was already spoken for: he had a girlfriend. Uschi and I had seen them on the street a few times; she was a lot taller than I. Uschi asked me if they were engaged. I said I didn't know.

Max also had a close relationship with the wife of an American farmer. She was an interesting and intelligent woman. Max made batiste scarves for her. During her visits to Dresden, she always stayed at an elegant hotel on Prager Strasse. That's where they first met. Max was standing outside the hotel observing things as artists do. She asked, "Excuse me, are you looking for someone?" And so their friendship began.

Whenever she was in Germany, the American woman met with Max. She brought him memorial coins and gold coins. I didn't know about those coins at the time, but Max's sister—the witch—knew about them, and she took them from him. That's why, later on, I wanted nothing to do with my husband's relatives. My husband had two nephews. They are both doctors—one a surgeon, the other a specialist in internal medicine. The mother of these boys, Max's sister, was a snobbish woman with strong fascist tendencies. I never got to know my father-in-law. Max's mother had died years before, which is why he moved from Breslau to Dresden.

Anyway, Max was very close to this American woman who was rolling in money. But I was a pretty slip of a thing and I just didn't worry about it. Max had fallen in love with me. At first I brushed him off. I didn't even bother showing up on some of our dates. But he had really fallen for me and always came back to his little one.

One fine day he came to me and said, "Do you know what? I've fallen in love with you and I've told my girlfriend about it." I had not heard from him in some time, so I thought it was all over. He said that he hadn't come around because he'd needed the time to break up with his girlfriend.

"I'm free. I'm at your disposal. We can be together forever now."

I was shocked—especially when he said "forever." Together forever? I was stunned. It had never occurred to me. I was still young, and he didn't even know that I was a Jew. I didn't exactly advertise it. He was blond, I was dark. I didn't say yes or no. I was speechless.

I still had my printing press—and then there was Max Eisenhardt, who supposedly wanted to marry me. He already had the money and the papers together. But he was too much of a coward. He wasn't a real man. He was spineless. Big promises, big beer: Slibowitz and Pilsener.

But Max Krause ... now there was a man.

4 Deportation and Return

After the four months in prison in 1933 for insulting the Führer, I was jailed again for a few weeks because of supposed irregularities with my documents. I was born in Dresden, so I had never needed a passport and had only my police registration certificate. My mother was married to a German, but I was considered Hungarian. Thanks to her bad German, she had registered me incorrectly everywhere. At first she registered me under the name of her first husband, Pollack. Then she had Samel adopt me. Under the new laws, the adoption was no longer valid; the Nazis annulled it. So even though I'd never visited the place in my life, I became a Hungarian citizen once again.

By the time I was released from jail, fascism was in its heyday. In 1934, I was once again taken to court for irregularities with my documents. I was convicted, but this time I was able to serve the sentence on probation. The authorities decided that I was to be deported to my "homeland" as soon as possible—that is, expelled over the border (toward Hungary) to Czechoslovakia.

One morning I was picked up by a police officer named Herbert Ossmann, who would come to play a big role in my life. I was supposed to have spent the night at Ostbahnstrasse where Max Krause had his studio apartment. Max had invited me to sleep at his place the night before. When I asked him why, he said, "I have an odd feeling."

During this time, I was often at Max's place. He was really happy about that because Otto Griebel and all the other artists who lived there wanted to get to know me. From time to time, I still had to go to my print shop. I had not yet signed it over to Eisenhardt, but it more or less belonged to him because Jews weren't allowed to own anything anymore. Eisenhardt always arranged things to suit himself. By then our friendship was over. I came and went as I pleased. My only remaining possession at the print shop was a large wicker trunk—my hope chest.

Many artists had such a trunk. I had bought mine with marriage in mind and used it to store my dowry collection: five hand towels, bedsheets bound together with ribbons, and dishtowels. In those days, you didn't just go into a shop and buy your dowry things all at once. Whenever I managed to save a couple of marks, I would go to Heckel & Partner and buy a few things. You never bought yourself a complete bedroom set. You went to a carpenter and bought a piece by a journeyman. You made friends with the carpenter in case he had another such piece. That's how you collected the furniture for your home, piece by piece, because the carpenter knew what he had already delivered to you and knew what fit.

Max Krause and I had grown very close by then. In the end, what brought us together was our shared political views. The house on Ostbahnstrasse had been built specifically for artists; it contained many large, beautiful studios. I would go to Max's and feel right at home. I couldn't live there myself because, as a Hungarian Jew, I was no longer officially registered; it would have been too risky. So I found myself a room nearby on Viktoria Strasse. There was a marriage broker's office in the building and so many people coming and going that I didn't stand out. The SA were marching everywhere at that time. I was living illegally in Dresden and was supposed to be expelled because of my previous convictions. I felt pretty secure in the room on Viktoria Strasse, so I had not stayed over at Max's that night.

The police officer, Herbert Ossmann, picked me up at my room on Viktoria Strasse at around five in the morning. Ossmann had taken part in a big shooting competition in Austria and won a prize as the best shot. He was one of Hitler's boys right from the start—a fanatic to the last breath. He began his career as police officer and duty officer at the police station on Portikusstrasse. Later he was an overseer in a Jewish ghetto. Actually, he was a good-looking man.

Ossmann picked me up and took me to the guardhouse at the train station. I spent long hours in a tiny cell. Finally, another police officer—an older man—approached me. "You're about to be picked up. Don't bother crying. Nothing is going to happen to you."

"So you say," I replied. "Are you married?"

Otto Griebel, circa 1927. (Otto Griebel, *Ich war ein Mann der Strasse. Lebenserinnerungen eines Dresdner Malers* [Dresden 1986, 2nd printing 1995], front cover.)

"Yes. I lead a respectable life and I am married."

"You know," I went on, "I have a funny feeling that I'm going to be thrown out of Dresden—out of Germany. You're never going to see me again. I have a key. It belongs to my boyfriend. He's one of the artists living at Ostbahnstrasse 1. That's just a couple of minutes from the main train station. I don't want to keep this key."

"Why do you even have that key?" he asked. "You were searched, weren't you?"

"Let's just say I found a very embarrassing hiding place for it."

The police officer laughed. "Okay, give it to me. I'll take it over there." These were dangerous times. Such an offer could have cost him his job and God knows what else.

He arrived at Ostbahnstrasse 1 to find all of the painters sitting there with Max. "I'm supposed to give you this key," he said. "Your girlfriend said it belonged to you." Max knew immediately what that meant—that I was to be deported. Otto Griebel and the other painters left, but Max ran to the train station and waved to me as I was leaving.

Ossmann took me by train to the Czech border. First we went to a restaurant to wait and see if everything was in place for my border crossing. All I had to do, I was told, was walk on over and just keep walking. But when I arrived on the Czech side of the border, I was approached by the border guard—a Yugoslav who spoke Czech. He asked where I was planning to go. I showed him my police registration certificate from Dresden. He looked at it and said I should go right back where I came from or else he would be obliged to put me in jail.

When he found out that I had not eaten all day, he sat me down on a rock and found a woman who brought her youngster with her. She gave me a loaf of fresh bread.

"I want to give you some good advice," he said. "Go back over there because if you don't I'll have to arrest you. This is Czech territory and you have no papers. You're hardly the first person I've given this advice to— it's going on every day and every hour—but you're the youngest one so far."

Not long after, I walked back to the German side of the border. It was dark by then. Herbert Ossmann was furious. As we stood by the Elbe River, it was obvious that he wanted to get rid of me as soon as possible. "Can you swim?" he asked. When I said no, he threw me into the water. I swam back to the bank. As he pulled me out, he said to me, "And you're a liar to boot."

He took me back to the restaurant at the border. I sat there in my dripping wet clothes on a circular bench surrounding a card table where skat was usually played, and I awaited my fate. It turned out that since the last train had already left, I was to spend the night there. Ossmann asked me how much money I had. "Thirty marks," I said.

The thirty marks would pay for my room—which was as sparse as it was cheap—and something to eat. The next day Ossmann would take me to another border crossing at Bad Schandau.

There was a steep set of stairs leading to my room. It had a bed, a chair, and a table with folding legs. I wanted to lock the door before turning in but discovered there was no key. So instead of taking off all my clothes, I removed my coat and hat and threw myself on the bed.

Over beer and schnapps, the landlord and Ossmann had cooked up a plan. I was not to be given a key. That night the two of them came up to my room and tore my clothes off. Ossmann was on the verge of raping me—he had everything out of his pants—when the landlady called out, "What is that racket? What's going on up there? Get down here this instant!"

I was yelling like someone being roasted alive, and that's why the landlady woke up. The landlord and Ossmann, both in a rage, left immediately.

The next morning at breakfast I met a man who was delivering The Freedom Struggle, the Nazi newspaper for the district of Saxony. The man, who delivered all the Nazi papers to the villages, sat at my table. It was just the two of us. From the thirty marks I still had money for a cup of coffee and a roll with butter.

After a while, the man spoke. "I'm going to take you over the border. It's going to work this time because I deliver the papers. You were handed over to me by Herbert Ossmann."

I scrutinized the man. There's a crooked number, I thought. My time in prison had given me a feel for such people. In any event, during the night I had come up with a plan. I always dream up my best plans at night.

After breakfast, Ossmann, the mailman, and I went to the train station. After Ossmann left, I asked the mailman, "Do you have children?"

"Yes," he said, "four of them."

"Do you want to earn some money?"

"Why? Do you have some hidden somewhere?"

"No, but I have a print shop and there's money there. If you take me back to Dresden, we can go there and I'll give you a few hundred marks. We can't talk here anymore. I'm hanging around the train station even though I'm supposed to have been deported. We're in the same boat. We have to keep it to ourselves. You say you took me over the border and that's that."

He agreed to the plan and fetched me clothing, high-heeled shoes, and a large hat. I put on a bit of makeup and did my hair differently. He brought me back to Dresden—to Ostbahnstrasse and Max Krause. Max wasn't at home, so I went to Otto Griebel's fine house at Pillnitzer Landstrasse 93. He wasn't home either, but his wife—Margarete—was there. She was breastfeeding her little son, Matthias, and was totally shocked.

"Janka! Are you crazy?" ("Janka" was the Hungarian version of "Johanna.") "I'm breastfeeding. My milk will block up on me. What on earth are you thinking?"

"Your milk isn't going anywhere, Gretel. I wasn't here. I was deported so I couldn't have been at your place. You don't have to be afraid. I'm here with someone I've promised money to."

"But how did you get back in? You're going to get us all into trouble."

"Don't be afraid. When Otto comes home, just tell him to send Max to the print shop right away. And remember, you never saw me."

"Okay, I'll do it," she said.

Gretel was glad when I left. They were not heroes. They all trembled, but I'm glad they only trembled. Later they were all called heroes.

Several hours later, Max Krause came to the print shop. The key I'd arranged to have delivered to him opened my hope chest. Max Eisenhardt would have had to destroy the trunk to get at the money inside, but he refused to let me have it—that is, until Max Krause threatened to throw him across the high-speed press. "You just used everybody and everything," he told Eisenhardt.

During my last stay in prison, Eisenhardt had sold all my dowry items. He sold my linen because he had debts all over the city. He was a live wire, that one, always up to something.

At last the mailman received his money. He was relieved to be rid of the situation. We shook hands. Done, over, fini. Max Eisenhardt kept the trunk; the key remained with Max Krause.

Now I was absolutely illegal in Dresden.

5 Our Unusual Wedding

Without a passport I couldn't go anywhere. I couldn't leave Germany. I had to go underground. Max Eisenhardt helped by taking me to his lover on Hopfgartenstrasse. His girlfriend's mother, a very nice woman, had a two-room apartment. She let me hide there for a couple of weeks. It was an old house with an outhouse, so I had to rig something up in the house or wait for nightfall and go outside hoping no one would see me.

In the meantime, Max Krause went to the Hungarian consulate on Beuststrasse, located in the part of Dresden called the Great Garden. Soon after, Dr. Stein—a Jewish man—provided me with a Hungarian passport. I couldn't use it right away because officially I had been deported. Still, for the first time in my life I had a passport.

Max Krause, Max Eisenhardt, and I waited until Easter—the time of year when Oberwiesenthal, a small Bohemian village on the border between Germany and Czechoslovakia, attracted many holiday skiers. Obviously, I couldn't just stroll across the border—so we hatched a plan. Armed to the teeth with packages of cigarettes, Max Krause approached the border guards on the German side. "Heil Hitler," he said. "How're you doing?" As he passed out cigarettes, he chatted about politics and all sorts of things. The guards fetched schnapps, and they all had a few drinks. I remained in the background the whole time.

Max Krause was a first-class fox. He went to the Czech side of the border and repeated the whole act. The Czechs were eager to get their hands on German cigarettes. Finally, he went over with me right behind him. The guards were in high spirits because of the alcohol and didn't notice me. I showed them my passport as if it were the most natural thing in the world.

Max Krause and Max Eisenhardt took me to the Slany Hotel on the border in Bohemia-Wiesenthal. So, I had made it over in one piece. Max Krause gave me rent money for half a year. I offered to do work, no matter what it was. I had to eat after all. They registered me as an assistant in the kitchen, but I was not allowed to work. I went increasingly into debt.

I used my time in another way. I studied the border. For an entire year, I lived in exile because my plans to return to Germany fell through. The fact is, Max Eisenhardt and I were contemplating a marriage of convenience, but in the end he wouldn't go through with it. Max Eisenhardt was no Max Krause.

In the meantime, the Sudeten-German Henlein arrived on the scene as Czechoslovakia's Nazi leader. So Germany had Hitler and Czechoslovakia had Henlein. Henlein and Hitler were one and the same.

Max Krause learned that Max Eisenhardt was abandoning me. "You know what?" he said to Eisenhardt. "You can fuck off and buy your own Slibowitz and Pilsener beer. If you're out of money, then go get yourself arrested. I've had it with you. I'm marrying Janka."

He proposed to me in Czechoslovakia. "Johanna, I've had enough of Eisenhardt. In eight weeks, the Nazis are implementing new regulations. We can't afford to wait any longer. I'm marrying you and we have to do it fast."

"No, you're not marrying me." I said, "because if you do, you're going to have so many problems. It'll wreck your life."

"I'm marrying you whether you want it or not," Max countered.

"You can't marry me. I have nothing." That gave him something to think about. But he just said, "I'll take care of everything. I've already got all the information."

As a member of the Red Mountain Climbers, Max knew many Czech and Yugoslavian mountain climbers, and he turned to them to find out how to go about the whole thing. Mountain climbers are a rare breed of people. They have a special camaraderie because they depend on one another for their very lives—just one mistake and a buddy could die. They're honest and have strong friendships that last a lifetime; in other words, they're great people. And while they appeared to go along with the state on the outside, on the inside they thought the opposite. They taught us some tricks that helped us to carry out our plan so that no one noticed a thing.

On top of that, Max had a fine comrade, an engineer in Prague, who advised him to see a certain lawyer and arrange for a dispensation. A dispensation meant that our marriage certificate would state that neither of us had any religious affiliation—that we were "undenominational." Nowhere on the certificate would the word "Jew" appear. But a dispensation that was recognized in Czechoslovakia cost a thousand marks, payable in Czech kronen. That was a lot of money, and it took Max a long time to earn it through his painting; in the end, he sold a seascape to a Nazi firm.

Max visited me regularly throughout the year. He took a big risk by bringing me banned newspapers and the like. I continued to study the border. On the Czech side there were three customs officers. One of them was a soldier whose name, funnily enough, was the word for "soldier"—Szoldat. I made friends with these border guards. Heavens, I wasn't as witless then as I am now in my old age! I was clever and checked out the best possible place for getting back over the border.

I didn't want to have anything to do with the Sudetenland Germans who were screaming "*Heim ins Reich*—Home into the German Reich!" Instead I was drawn to Czechs like the mailman and the border guards. These were my friends. I had the privilege of sitting at their table. At that time, the Czechs retained a bit of power. But the Sudetenland Germans were on the march with their swastika flags.

A year went by and I was getting uneasy. For a period of about eight weeks, I heard nothing more. No one came. I was slowly losing my nerve. I started thinking of ways to get back to Germany. One strategy involved a bus at the border that was used by sports people from Joachimsthal returning to Dresden. So I came up with a scheme that went against everything we had planned up until that point. It was a terrible plan, but I was at the end of my tether.

Just as I about to put my plan into action, Max Krause arrived as if destiny had called him. "I've never heard such a dumb thing in my life," he said after I revealed my scheme. "How could you? When I say I'm going to marry you, how can you even consider such a thing? Aren't you ashamed of yourself?"

He carried on in this vein awhile. Then he travelled to Prague to pick up our dispensation. He returned from Prague with the dispensation and the marriage certificate. "How should we arrange for the wedding?" he asked the landlord. "I want to marry Janka here." The people at the border weren't stupid; they knew what was up. In fact, they had put something aside for us just for this moment. The landlord said that a wedding with German witnesses would not be possible. We didn't want that anyway. That's why all the names on our wedding certificate are Czech names. There was the landlord, Mr. Slany; the postmaster and postmistress; and a border guard. They were our witnesses. It's in front of those good people that we made our vows.

We didn't want a big ceremony because we had no money. "At my hotel, you are going to celebrate your wedding," the landlord protested. "We'll take a collection for it." So, on October 21, 1935, we were married in a chapel in Joachimsthal. Our Czech friends then treated us to a reception in the Slany Hotel. At the reception, there was wonderful food with traditional Czech dumplings. Instead of a wedding dress, I wore a fashionable dark blue skirt and a white blouse. I was such an enthusiastic dancer that some of the guests couldn't figure out who my husband was. We danced until dawn and toasted to a happy marriage with Slibowitz and beer.

The next day my husband talked about returning to Germany. "The dispensation on the marriage certificate and the Hungarian passport won't be enough to get you back into Germany," he told me. "I'll have to offer cigarettes and schnapps again. You know the border by now. You'll have to go to the best spot where the border takes twists and turns, where it's narrow to cross and the water isn't so deep."

So it had come to this—another illegal crossing. I had a passport and could have gone to other countries, but I couldn't return to Germany because I had been deported from there. I could have stayed in Czechoslovakia but living in a Czech village without speaking the language fluently would have been too difficult.

We planned every last detail. Max paid all my debts, including those I had incurred in Bohemia-Wiesenthal. He didn't earn much as an artist, so in the evenings he worked as a waiter. In the taverns, you could earn whatever the ladies and the rich people were prepared to give you. They were usually quite generous, and Max looked good so he got lots of tips. But he was always exhausted because it was very stressful having to buzz about from one tavern to another in order to earn money.

The Czechs didn't require a huge sum, since I had already made a partial payment. But protocol demanded that we ask what we still owed. Max

Země: Land: .....Česká. - .Böhmen...............................   11916|142.

Polit. okres: .Jáchymov.
Polit. Bezirk: St.Joachimsthal.

Výpis - Auszug

z knihy sňatků okresního úřadu v .St. Joachi...
aus dem Eheregister der Bezirksbehörde in .St. Joachi...thal.

svazek ./. , ročník 1935 , strana 32
Band .... Jahrgang .... Seite ...

		ženicha — des Bräutigams	nevěsty -- der Braut
1.	Řadové číslo knihy sňatků Post-Zahl des Eheregisters	10	
2.	Rok, měsíc a den, kdy bylo manželství uzavřeno Jahr, Monat u. Tag der geschlossenen Ehe	21. října Oktober 1935	
3.	Jméno a příjmení Vor- und Familienname	Max Konrád Krause	Albine Johanna Lindner -ová
4.	Rodiště a domovská příslušnost v den sňatku Geburtsort und Heimatzuständigkeit am Tage der Eheschließung	Vratislava - Breslau Dražďany - Dresden	Dražďany - Dresden Budapešt
5.	Zaměstnání Beschäftigung	Malíř - Kunstmaler	bez-ohne
6.	Bydliště Wohnort	Dražďany - Dresden Ostbahnstrasse 1 a	Č.-Wiesenthal Hotel "Slaný"
7.	Den, měsíc a rok narození (stáří) Tag, Monat und Jahr der Geburt (Alter)	17.II.1907	23.X.1907
8.	Jeou-li svobodní anebo byli-li již ve svazku manželském Ledig oder bereits verheiratet gewesen	svobodný - ledig	svobodná -ledig
9.	Náboženské vyznání – bez vyznání Konfession — Konfessionslos	bez - konfessionslos	bez - konfessionslos
10.	Jméno, příjmení a zaměstnání rodičů ženicha a nevěsty Vor- u. Familienname, Beschäftigung der Eltern der Brautleute	Georg Reinhold Krause Selma, roz. Grosserová ./.	./. Johanna Lindner-ová ./.
11.	Jméno, příjmení, zaměstnání a bydliště svědků Zeugen, Vor- und Familienname, der Beruf und Wohnort derselben	Vilém-Wilhelm Slaný, Č.-Wiesenthal. Josef Hrnčíř, úředník, Jáchymov-St.Joachimsthal	
12.	Jméno a hodnost služební osob úředních, před nimiž ženich a nevěsta slavně prohlásili, že přivolují k manželství Namen und Dienstcharakter der Amtspersonen, vor welchen die feierliche Erklärung der Einwilligung zur Ehe abgegeben wurde	JUC Josef Majk, komisař pol.správy, Jáchymov. František Tutach, kanc.oficiant, Jáchymov.	
13.	Listiny, jimiž překážky vzešlé byly zrušeny Urkunden, wodurch die vorgekommenen Hindernisse behoben wurden	./.	
14.	Poznámky Anmerkungen	./.	

Okresní úřad v .Jáchymově
Bezirksbehörde in St.Joachimsthal

dne
am ....21. října.........1935

Za okresního hejtmana
Komisař polit. správy:
Für den Bezirkshauptmann
Kommissar d. polit. Verwaltung

Johanna and Max's Czech/German-language marriage certificate, dated October 21, 1935, and issued by the district administration in Joachimsthal. It states that the couple are "konfessionslos" (undenominational). (Estate of Johanna Krause.)

had already said his goodbyes when the landlord from the Slaney Hotel came up to him and asked, "Tell me, who is really with the young woman? Mr. Eisenhardt or you?"

"Oh, let sleeping dogs lie," Max said. The landlord laughed and gave Max a punch on the shoulder, like men do. The case was closed, and he wished us the best of luck.

We needed all the luck we could get because as I waited to cross the green border at my chosen spot, the German soldiers from German-Oberwiesenthal started to patrol the area with their dogs. I saw my husband approach them and start to chat. This sight was reassuring, but because of the dogs I had to slip into the water and wait it out. If a dog heard you splash, you had to do the dead man's float until it went by. That's what I did. I had no choice because those dogs were trained to hunt down people even if they were far away.

In the water, I lost my sense of direction and missed the narrow spot, the best place for crossing the border comfortably. I ended up having to scale a steep bank. I really didn't think I would make it. Where I got the strength to climb that cliff I don't know. People do unbelievable things in an emergency. I must have had a guardian angel helping me.

I finally made it to the top. Max arrived and we got on the bus. I was soaking wet. The driver stared at me. Max told him that I had fallen into the water by accident. The driver could have been a diehard Nazi for all we knew. But he lived near the border, and although he must have smelled a rat, he allowed me on the bus.

We sat at the front of the bus near the driver. Suddenly I had to throw up. I vomited over everything. I just couldn't stop myself.

Max was furious. "Did you have to go and do that?" He swore at me, then said to the driver, "Here, take this five marks and give me a rag. I'll wipe this up."

"I'll do it myself," the driver said.

Of course, five marks meant more back then than it does today. Even so, the driver acted very decently.

6 Imprisoned for "Defiling the Race"

Freshly married and with a new name, I returned to Dresden at my husband's side. From now on I was Johanna Krause. We moved in together and the artists at the Ostbahnstrasse studio welcomed us. We didn't have money for bread, but that wasn't a problem. Artists stick together. They brought us food.

The studio was about thirty square metres and the room next to it about twenty square metres. We bought ourselves a brass four-poster bed and a washstand with a mirror and commode. Max's American friend kept sending him dollars for the batiste scarves. He used the money to buy me a sealskin jacket with an opossum collar and a hat with a fine veil (all fashionable at the time). He also got me stockings with little roses and garters, and a pair of flat Salamander shoes—usually I wore heels—because he wanted to go hiking with me.

Those were the happiest days of my life. They didn't last long.

In 1936, my husband and I were imprisoned for "defiling the race." In their efforts to exterminate Jews, the Nazis had come up with all sorts of measures. But not everything had worked out as they wanted, so they devised a new scheme for separating me from my "Aryan" husband. Because they couldn't annul our marriage without consequences, the Nazis decided that—according to German law—Max had married a foreigner.

On June 12, a policeman and policewoman came to Ostbahnstrasse and rang the bell. They told us to get dressed because they were taking us to a hearing at police headquarters. Of course, we went with them; I was trembling with fear. We were sent to the prison on Schiessgasse for eight weeks. The treatment there was fine. I got along with the guards. I could see the human qualities in these women. We gave the guards nicknames.

Police headquarters and prison on Schiessgasse, where Johanna was imprisoned under both the Nazis and the Communists. Photo circa 1975. (Saxon State and University Library Dresden, German Photothek #184025. Photo by Rolf Heselbarth.)

The one we called "the rat" was a very small person and a bit hateful. Knowing this, I was extra nice to her.

The food was not the greatest and you had to submit to the system. You had to be disciplined. You had to play by the rules and behave decently. And, of course, you had to be clever; you had to concentrate totally on what was coming up next.

In jail, I knitted for the soldiers. This earned me a slight advantage, an extra piece of bread or recognition for myself and my work. I had nothing to change into, not even an extra shirt, and I wasn't given anything either. I was registered as a special case, as if I had murdered an entire family.

One day they came and got me. "Today you're going to see your husband," I was told.

"Am I being released now?"

"It depends."

I was to be taken with my husband to the Jewish community centre, because after eight weeks they had to finally prove that we had "defiled the race." They knew that I was a Jew, but the laws for "defiling the race" were complicated—a lot of fine print. In the end, it came down to the question: Who is a Jew and who isn't? The Nazis decided that if you were registered with the Jewish community, there was no turning back—you were a Jew.

It was a huge relief to see my husband again. He had been held with male prisoners in another cell.

The guard spoke to my husband. "You are being taken to the Jewish community centre. If your wife is listed with them, there's no hope for you. You should prepare yourself mentally for this possibility." This meant: concentration camp!

"Oh my God," I said to Max. "I'm registered for sure. We're finished."

"Don't lose hope," he countered. "Think about it. Your name has often been mixed up."

We finally arrived at the community centre. Each community, be it religious or political, was obliged to keep lists of its members, and each community had a person charged with this task. In the Jewish community, this person was a Jewish man who was later picked up by the Russians and killed because he was a traitor who had turned many Jews over to the Nazis.

At the community centre, this man looked at me in apparent confusion. As we sat before him, he searched his thick book for the name Pollack. It wasn't there because my mother's first husband, Pollack, was dead by the time I was born. I then gave him the name Samel, and it wasn't in the book either. The man did not continuing searching, whether by chance or intention I do not know. Because I had been an illegitimate child, I was registered under "Lindner," my mother's maiden name. If this man had been a swine and persisted, he definitely would have found me. Then again, in recent years no one from the Jewish community had bothered about me, and I hadn't bothered about them because I had a criminal conviction. I think what happened is that my mother, in her addle-brained way and thanks to her bad German, had inadvertently helped me by messing up the entry.

In any case, Max and I were free.

7 Forced Labour and Sterilization

After we were released from jail, my husband worked again as an artist. I tried my luck as a waitress until the Gestapo came after me.

As someone fresh out of jail, I couldn't exactly sign up for *Kraft durch Freude* ("Strength through Joy"), a Nazi organization that ran nice steamboat tours where I could have worked as a waitress. Also, I had not done a lot of waitressing and, as a Jew, I definitely could not take any sort of training. Good heavens! No way.

But we needed the money, so I scoured the help-wanted ads for temp jobs without contracts. That's how I started. But I still paid taxes; it would have been dreadful not to have paid taxes. In the records, you could see my dates of employment as a temp worker. It was a start.

I made a good impression as a job applicant. I was young and thin, and I didn't have a hunched back like I do now. I flitted down the street like a fairy. I had a good figure and an honest face. Being vain, I worked hard to keep up my appearance; I could make a pretty scarf out of a scrap of left-over cloth. Thanks to my looks and gift for gab, I was hired by various establishments, including a tavern. The customers in the tavern acted more decently than the customers in the bourgeois places who acted like pigs.

One of those upscale places was the Bräustübel on Carusstrasse. They had five types of beer (Kulmbacher, Pilsener, DAB, and two others) that I had to learn. But I had a good memory and was good at adding up the bills. If something was amiss, I noticed right away. Being able to calculate correctly was essential; the other skills you could learn. Luckily, I had trained as a saleswoman and, being a fast learner, I could pick all the rest.

Next I worked at Raps, a solidly middle-class restaurant on Bankstrasse. I told the owner that I wanted to work there because I'd heard it was a decent establishment. "I'm married," I added, "but I'm married to an artist and so I need to earn money."

Waitressing was poorly paid in general. The restaurant owners paid your health insurance but everything else you earned on commission. If you worked efficiently, and were polite and honest, you could make a living. I was not the type who slept with the customers. The owner appreciated this because he didn't want his restaurant to develop a bad reputation. And so he hired me.

Like every such restaurant, it had a clubroom. The clubroom was used mostly by state prosecutors and judges. They wore monocles and stiff ties, and each had his own beer stein—elegant and expensive painted ceramic mugs with pewter covers. Each customer had his own place to sit and a sponge for playing skat (a German card game with bidding). The sponge had to be kept wet so that the customer could play a good hand of cards. The first part of the evening was calm enough. But after they had finished playing, they would get in high spirits and tell dirty jokes and slap me on the bum. I forbade them to do so.

After a couple of weeks, one of the customers said, "Hey, she doesn't look so Aryan now, does she?"

I went straight to my boss. "Excuse me, but I don't feel comfortable here. I thought this was a decent place. I can't allow all this touching to go on." I finished my calculations for the night, hung up my apron, and left. It was too dangerous.

In 1938, a new law came out. The Reich Chamber of Culture issued a list of actors, painters, and sculptors who were married to Jews. We were on the list, as were Hans Grundig (I have some of his paintings) and Lea Grundig.

We were ordered to appear before the officials. Christian husbands were firmly advised to divorce their Jewish wives.

"I am not going to divorce my wife," my husband said. "You can do what you want—but no, no, NO!"

"How can you just throw your life away like that?" they asked. "You aren't going to get any more work. You won't be able to paint any longer. Consider what's in store for you—banned from practising your profession!"

So Max, because of "political unreliability and being related to a Jew,"

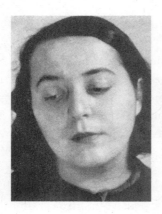

Lea Grundig, a member of the circle of artists to which Max belonged, 1932. (*Dresdner Hefte* 45, no. 14 [1996]: 73.)

was shut out of the Reich Chamber of Culture and banned from practising his profession as a painter.

But Hans Grundig continued working as a painter. I was astounded. "You aren't allowed to paint anymore," I said to my husband. "You won't be able to sell your work. But Hans can. Maybe Hans and Lea divorced. I never see them together now."

"Johanna, you're always right. You've got a certain intuition about these things," my husband said. "But I just can't believe it."

Not long after, as Max was giving an acquaintance his easel, I was looking out our studio window. "Come quick!" I called to Max. "There are two police officers with Hans and Lea. They're being picked up!"

The two of them were briefly imprisoned. Lea was able to immigrate to what later became Israel. Her father, who owned a large business on Grossen Brüdergasse, put all his energy and money into helping Lea. He paid a huge amount for her bail. Lea shared a studio with Hans Grundig on Ostbahnstrasse. She was a painter as well, and although she wasn't as talented as Hans, she learned a lot from him.

In 1941, my husband was drafted. He was the only thing that stood between me and deportation. He had to work in the kitchen and in construction—the kind of work reserved for people who were a thorn in the Nazis' side but the Nazis couldn't get at them directly. Max belonged to this group because he had married a Jew.

"Chin up, Johanna," he said before he left. "I know what you're thinking. But you don't need to be afraid. Don't get into any trouble. I'll be back in three or four months."

Gestapo im Haus (*Gestapo in the House*), drypoint by Lea Grundig, 1934. (*Lea Grundig, Jüdin, Kommunistin, Graphikerin* [Berlin, exhibition catalogue of the Laden Gallery, 1996], p. 23.)

I accompanied him to the train station. I couldn't stop crying. I couldn't believe that he could get out of this one. Still, his words consoled me somewhat and gave me a bit of courage before the inevitable deportation. I knew that once the men were drafted, they came and got the wives in order to separate the "Aryan" blood from the Jewish. Many couples committed suicide at that point because they couldn't bear to be separated.

So my husband was drafted and learned how to shoot. As I continued my life on Ostbahnstrasse, Max thought of ways of getting out of there. He had always had lung trouble. At one point, he caught a bad chest cold and ended up in the sick bay. He was taken to a special lung clinic in Adorf. While there, he went to a patient who had full-blown TB and infected himself with phlegm. After falling ill with TB himself, Max was taken to a military hospital. He wrote me a letter saying that he would probably continue serving if he recovered.

But that didn't happen. Four months later, I heard the sound of pebbles being thrown against the window. I was terrified. That's it, I thought, they're coming to get you.

It was the middle of the night. I went to the door and looked through the keyhole. Suddenly I heard my husband's deep voice. "Johanna, for heaven's sake, open up sweetie. Your Max is back."

There he was, in person, at the door. At first I thought he was only on leave. But then he showed me his release papers with his photo declaring that he was "unfit for military service" because of severe TB. In fact, after seeing doctors in Dresden, he had to return to the clinic in Adorf for a while. But the main thing was, he was back. I was so overjoyed that I was speechless.

"Why are you so surprised?" he asked me.

"Max, I really can't believe it."

"But I told you I'd be back in three or four months. And didn't I keep my word? A promise is a promise." He was so happy.

I couldn't even answer him. The whole thing was just too much for me. "You've done something to yourself," I said finally, "and it could turn out badly for you and your health.

"Okay, it was pretty disgusting," he agreed. "But if I had stayed in the military and couldn't be here to help you.... Don't worry. It's going to be fine."

That's the story with Max's military service. It meant we could stay together and, during the worst years anyway, I wouldn't be taken away. In those difficult times that followed, Max took the load off me.

Every month Jews had to go to Johannesstrasse to pick up the Jewish ration cards. Because Max was "tainted" by a Jew, our block leader—that is, the Nazi Party official who was in charge of our neighbourhood—was not allowed to deliver the regular ration cards to us. In our artists' house there were no traitors, no Nazis, and so this fellow could be trusted.

He rang our bell. "Mr. Krause, what's going on here?" he asked. "You're tall and blond. Why can't I bring you your food ration cards?"

"Because I'm married to a Jew," my husband replied.

The two of them talked for a long time. The block leader seemed to be quite smitten with Max; I was amazed that such a thing could exist. In the end, we received ration cards for Jews with the "J" marked on them. Of course, these cards didn't get you the same amount of rations as did the cards issued to "Aryans"—and certain items were left out altogether. Plus, each month you were afraid that you wouldn't be given the card at all because that would mean that your deportation date had arrived.

Luckily for us, a Doctor Dülz lived in our house with his niece, Susanna Freund. She had to do service as a nurse, but her true profession was painting miniatures. After work, she would bring us bread and butter. The soldiers she cared for had ample supplies. When they had to return to the front, they would give her their ration cards. "We can't use them anymore," they would tell her. "At the front we get even better rations."

Susanna always brought us something. Max loved the cigarillos she gave him. Once in a while, she would bring a bottle of schnapps, so we were really doing all right.

In the meantime, I had begun working in another restaurant. One day an elegant man came in and spoke to the owner. "That waitress you have—she's attractive. I could use her services at my bar on New Year's. My bartender is sick and, besides, he's not been bringing in any money." The owner told him to ask me himself, so the man approached me and asked if I'd be interested in working at his bar for four days. I replied that I had never worked at a bar before and would need some training. I also said that my husband was an artist, so I could use the extra money. "What you earn here in four weeks, you'll earn at my place in a day," the man promised.

He asked me if I owned an evening gown. I told him about a long black gown with wide sleeves and red lining that an actress had given me. It was rippled at the bosom. "Okay," he said, acknowledging my fashion know-how, "then choose a nice flower for your hair and come to my bar. I have

Max Krause's discharge certificate. (Estate of Johanna Krause.) *Translation opposite.*

Military Registration Number: DresdenI 02 / 11 / 39 / 10

Police Registration Station	Military District Commando
Dresden	Dresden 1

Discharge Certificate

[*Photo of Max Krause & Stamp of the District Military Commando*]

The <u>Painter</u>
Profession, First and Last Names

<u>Max Krause</u>
Born on Feb. 17, 1902, in Breslau

Is fully unfit for military service in the *Wehrmacht*. He can no longer be called up for service.

<u>Dresden,</u>   <u>Feb. 1, 1941</u>
Place mustered   Date

The District Police Authorities   The District Military Commander

---

Text of Max Krause's discharge certificate.

an offer for you. You know how there are thirty-five glasses in a bottle of cognac?"

"Actually, there are only thirty-two," I said.

"You get my drift," he laughed. "All right, thirty-two—but that's if you pour exactly and don't cheat me. So, you get a bottle of cognac and you pay me for each glass. Next you go downstairs, walking like the ladies do— smart, stylish, with a bit of a wiggle. You go to the kitchen and fetch your- self a tray with lemons, sugar, and ground coffee beans. Then you go upstairs to the bar. The sugar and whatnot, I provide. We'll even cut your lemons for you if you want. And when you sell the *Nikolaschkas*, the schnapps, that's your money. You just have to pay me for the bottle of co- gnac."

Right away I knew it was a fantastic offer. Even so, I told him I would have to discuss it with husband and give him an answer the next day.

"She's demanding, isn't she?" the man said to the owner. "Not really," the owner replied. "She's just a bit guarded and careful. She keeps a low profile. But I can't complain."

That evening I spoke with Max. "It's your choice," he said, "but we're two months behind in our rent. It'd be great to take care of some of our debts." The rent for our big studio apartment on Ostbahnstrasse was 176 marks; the studio covered the entire floor of the building and included an extra living room. "Ask him if I can pick you up," Max suggested, "and be there when you do your accounts for the night so the men don't bug you."

At the restaurant the next evening, the elegant man asked me if I had made up my mind. "Yes," I said, "but my husband would like to pick me up." So I started the extra job and earned a lot of money. "You're cheating, aren't you," my husband said. "You're mixing something in." But I wasn't, as it happened; I was making all that money from the *Nikolaschkas*. In any event, we managed to pay off all our debts and even had money left over. We were out of the woods.

In those days, you had to make the most of every opportunity. So, my husband would go to our butcher shop on Webergasse. The butcher was gay. My husband wasn't gay but he would go there anyway. At the meat counter, he would ask for a modest hundred grams of this and that and a couple of wieners. The butcher would look my husband in the eye and Max would give a little something back, though making sure it stayed on a no-nonsense level. So the butcher always prepared a large package of meat for him. Sometimes I would stand on the corner nearby just to see the butcher come out of the shop and watch Max as he walked away. Then I would duck behind the next house so I wouldn't be seen. Anyway, that earned us good food once a week.

My husband was careful not to let his encounters with the butcher get out of hand. He never went into the shop when it was empty; there were always other customers around. One time the butcher snuck in a message with the meat. I don't know what it said. I suspect it was a love note. My husband needed that. We both needed it. It was one of our tricks.

My job at the bar ended after New Year's. I started another waitressing job that I found through the classified ads. The permanent staff I was replacing would return after sick leave. That's how it was.

My last job was in a small tavern that was part of a hotel on Palmstrasse. The owner was a woman named Else Bagehorn. Her husband had died, so she was on her own and looking for honest employees. I never cheated her, and we got along very well. Later I found out that I'd been on probation. I never noticed. I worked for her for about three months, and I still have the letter of recommendation she gave me.

In those days, everyone was involved in some sort of illicit business. While Else worked in her office I was at the counter serving the customers.

After the war when I had problems with the communists, people would say, "They were doing shady deals too." But that was hogwash. First of all, everyone was involved, and second, they were doing a lot worse things then we ever did.

So as I said, everyone was engaged in shady deals. To get by, Else Bagehorn bamboozled her customers. She was also a member of the Nazi Party, but only because she had to be in order to keep her business. Her heart wasn't in it or she would never have helped me out. She knew who I was and found out quickly enough what sort of pressure we were under. That's why she bought a painting from my husband; unfortunately, it was destroyed during the bombing of Dresden in February 1945.

One day the Nazis approached Else. "Did you know that this waitress of yours is a Jew?" they asked.

"What? No way!" Else answered. "My husband is dead and I need someone to work with me in the office. Johanna is totally honest. She works alone at the counter. I paid a man to keep an eye on her to make sure she wasn't cheating me. He counted every cent that went in and out, and it was always exact. I don't need him anymore. The woman is perfectly honest."

"But she's a Jew," the men said.

"No, she can't be," Else said. "I am a National Socialist. I would have noticed that. Jews are cheaters, and Johanna is totally honest."

It didn't matter. The men removed me from the restaurant. They swore at me. How could I, a Jew, dare to serve "Aryan" customers? That's how I ended up in forced labour in a steam laundry on Kreischaer Strasse in Dresden-Strehlen. After the war, Else Bagehorn helped us a lot. She lent us money and helped me with my business.

The workers at the Strehlen Steam Laundry received clear instructions. "We're getting a Jew in here. No one is to hold private conversations with her. Don't speak to her at all unless it has something to do with the work." I was not allowed to go out with my fellow employees, and I couldn't bring my wash from home as all the others were permitted to do. Basically, everything connected with me was forbidden.

The introductory speech given by the Nazis backfired. My colleagues were all good to me. "What do you do with your wash?" one woman asked me. "I hardly have time for it," I replied. There were no permanent-press clothes back then. Instead there was linen, cotton, or damask, and everything had to be pressed—the shirts, the pants, the underwear. In those days, men wore proper underwear with buttons; there were lots of jokes about the underwear because men looked kind of funny in it, but washing it was hard work all the same.

"Bring everything you have to wash in a bag," the woman said to me. "Your sheets and everything. Put the bag right there. I'll empty it, and you can take everything back home again at night." Everyone did something. One colleague washed my dirty laundry, while the next ironed and another folded. It went from hand to hand, and they just acted as if it were their own laundry. They put the clean laundry back in my bag in the corner, and even carried it with them to the streetcar. I could relax at home because the wash was done.

The relationship with my colleagues was fabulous. However, no one was allowed to notice that. I acted as if I didn't know their names. I never spoke to them directly. But without their help, I would never have survived there.

Then they put me on a fast pressing machine. It was an old machine, and we used it to press the soldiers' dungarees. They were made of a type of linen that was very difficult to press. I had to work this machine for eight hours every day of the week. I was short and small and not so young anymore. Pushing the heavy machine up and down was very stressful. I had to adjust. I could carry heavy loads—I was used to carrying a tray of beer or food—but this was something else.

What was going to become of me? I never stopped asking myself this question. I was not the type of person who could work, get paid, and just get on with my life. I was a person who didn't have a clue what the next day would bring.

One day I started to cry. My small body was giving me hell. I was pregnant. To conceal it, I had tied myself into a corset. The bars of the corset dug painfully into my breasts. They were releasing milk already because I was quite advanced. I had stuffed a cloth in there to hide the wetness.

A colleague approached me. "What's up with you? You've been crying all day. Are you in pain? You're not pregnant, are you? You've put on so much weight." I didn't answer because I didn't want to lie. "You can tell me," she insisted.

"God almighty," I whispered to her. "I was brought here by the Gestapo!"

"Oh, you don't have to worry. Our boss is a woman; she'll arrange everything. If you can't work on that fast press anymore, then you can fold the wash and your difficulties will be over."

She meant well, but I didn't want her help. Despite this, she went to the boss. "Could we put the little one on folding clothes?" she asked her. "She's pregnant. Everyone can see that it's torture for her. We can take on her duties in shifts."

The boss was shocked. "She's what? Pregnant? That can't be!"

"It's true," my colleague answered. "She's been wrapping herself, so the work is doubly hard. That's why she's crying."

"I have to ask the Gestapo," the boss said.

Shortly after, someone from the Gestapo came to my machine. "Heil Hitler! Too lazy to work, eh? You don't even know what work is. Be happy that you, as a Jew, get to work for our soldiers!" He started hitting and kicking me.

"If you're married," I told him, "you try working this press eight hours a day."

"So that's it," he said. "You're pregnant too, you Jewish pig. I suppose you want pregnancy leave? And pregnancy ration cards. Ha! We'll get rid of it fast enough."

One morning they came in a car to get me. The car had blinds that were drawn, so I didn't know at first where I was going. I was taken to a doctor on Kaitzerstrasse in the Plauen Quarter, a part of Dresden with many villas. I was given medicine that produced cramps and then operated on. The baby was delivered by Caesarean section. It was already seven-and-a-half months old, fully formed, and would have lived if nature had been allowed to take its course.

"It was a boy," the nurse told me after the operation. "You're still young," she added in an attempt to console me. "You can still have many children."

She must have been in the dark about what was really going on there because years later I learned that, in addition to giving me the forced abortion, they had sterilized me. I had wanted to have ten children and now I couldn't have even one. And my husband? He couldn't do anything. He was told that I would be right back, but I lay there in a terrible state. I wasn't given anything to eat or drink, and it was four or five days before they took me home in a car. I was half dead.

Johanna's workbook from the Nazi period, with an entry showing that she worked at Adolf Bauer's cardboard factory just before her deportation. (Estate of Johanna Krause.)

Uns ist bekannt und wir versichern, dass
Frau Krause nur ca. 14 Tage bei uns be-
schäftigt war. Die Gestapo teilte uns mit,
dass Frau Krause aufgrund Ihrer Festnahme
an Ihren Arbeitsplatz nicht zurückkehrt.

Adolf Bauer
Fabrik und Lager für Apotheken-
Buchdruck - Kartonagen - Papi
Dresden A 4
Andreas - Schubert - Str. 12

Signed statement from Adolf Bauer concerning Johanna's arrest. (Estate of Johanna Krause.) *Translation:* We can attest that Mrs. Krause only worked approximately 14 days at our factory. The Gestapo told us that Mrs. Krause would not be returning to her workplace because of her arrest. (signed) Adolf Bauer, Factory and Warehouse for Apothecaries, Printers, Cartons, Address: Andreas-Schubert Str. 12

The women at the laundry didn't intend anything bad. They didn't know that Nazism was so vicious. In the 1990s, the abortion of my child was officially recognized as murder because the child could have lived.

After the operation, I was transferred to the Adolf Bauer cardboard factory on Neue Gasse. There was one section for Jews and another section for Jews, "mixed race," and Christians; I was in the latter section. The work wasn't particularly difficult, but once again I had to adjust to a totally new setting. Even worse, I was never paid so I had nothing to eat. We were supposed to earn about fifty-eight cents an hour, but after two or three weeks working there I'd not seen a red cent, and we needed the money desperately.

After the war, I tried to get the money Bauer owed me. I was told to make an appearance. There was a letter stating that I had earned the money. My husband went to Bauer and asked him for the money. But Bauer refused, saying he had already paid me.

It was Adolf Bauer who saw to it that I was sent to a concentration camp. He was a member of the SS and a Gestapo informant. He sent many artists to the camps. It was already too much for him that we were Jews, let alone that we were good-looking. He believed that Jews shouldn't be allowed to wear nice clothing. The average-looking Jews could keep their jobs, but anyone who stood out in a crowd, was their own person, or contradicted him in any way were deported. For example, there was a Jewish actress who had worked for the state theatre and been caught smoking a cigarette during the break. All the attractive women were gotten rid of right away. That's how he operated.

Adolf Bauer was a sadist.

Years after the war ended, I found myself in the Jewish community centre sitting next to the second wife of Victor Klemperer, who wrote about Adolf Bauer in his diaries. At one point during our conversation, she said that Adolf Bauer had saved many Jews.

"You weren't there," I replied angrily. "Adolf Bauer was with the SS and he is supposed to have helped Jews? It was Bauer who started the process of sending me to the camps. But the dead cannot speak."

8 In Prison in Dresden

Two weeks after I started working at the Adolf Bauer cardboard packaging factory, I was ordered to report to the Gestapo headquarters on Bismarckstrasse. "Do you know what?" I said to Max. "I have the feeling that if I go there I'm never coming back."

"I'll come with you, Johanna. You haven't broken the law."

"Maybe I took some food to someone. Maybe someone squealed on me. I really don't know. But I didn't steal anything and I haven't broken any law. Yet somehow I have the feeling I should get out of here."

"I'll go with you," Max simply repeated.

I told him then that when I had worked at Else Bagehorn's place I'd been in contact with some people from Poland and Czechoslovakia who worked at a slaughterhouse. They often brought me wieners and cuts of meat. Else had warned me about them. That's why I was so scared now.

"You've got to hide me, Max."

"Are you crazy? They would turn this place upside down to find you. They would check out all our acquaintances. A lot of people would be in trouble. You haven't broken the law."

So I went to the Gestapo with Max. "Nothing's going to happen," he said as I entered the building alone. "I'll be right here waiting here for you."

I had with me the wonderful purse that my husband had bought me to cheer me up. It was made of a fine leather that resembled crocodile— very modern. I had been to the Gestapo many times before and had observed how the women who worked there would tuck their purses under their arms as they went about their business.

Dresden's main train station, 1926. To the left is Bismarckstrasse, future site of the Gestapo headquarters. (Saxon State and University Library Dresden, German Photothek #304975. Photo by Walter Hahn.)

I climbed the stairs and headed to the "Jewish Section." I knew the three men sitting there: Schmidt, Klemm, and Müller. Mr. Schmidt was the Gestapo detective superintendent who was responsible for transports. He and his wife hated Jews, as did the head secretary, Mr. Klemm, and Rudolf Müller, who was known as "Jews' Müller." The second I entered the room, I was whacked across the head and told to wait outside. I had excellent hearing and overheard a woman say through the door, "I've already dictated the case about Auschwitz. First she stays a couple of weeks at the headquarters where she can rot, and then she's off to Auschwitz."

When I heard that I put my purse under my arm as I'd seen the women do and I hurried out of there. My husband was waiting outside.

"Let's go! We have to get out of here. They're getting rid of me! Come on!"

Max didn't believe it. He tried to calm me down, so we were still standing there when the doorman came out. "Thank God you're still here! Please come in." He pushed us both inside. I could have escaped, but I don't know how far I would have got.

Once we were inside, they grabbed my husband and threw him into a bunker. They almost broke his back and forced him to repeat over and over, "I'm going to divorce that Jewish pig." After spending a few days in a cell, my badly beaten husband was allowed to return home. They treated him terribly. But I only learned about all that much later.

I was held in a cell at the police headquarters. I was there a long time—it seemed like forever—as they discussed my case and which camp I should be sent to. Because I had a previous conviction, I was placed with the communist prisoners. My cellmate was Hildegard Lehmann, a city councillor and communist who had met with Ernst Thälmann. From her I learned all about the Thälmann story.

In my opinion, the Thälmann people made a fatal error when they organized in a large group. The Scholls, the brother and sister, made the same mistake and were also captured. If they had gone it alone and not told anyone, they might still be alive today. In a big group, someone always cracks and talks. The interrogations were brutal. You had to be incredibly strong and have nerves of steel. The Gestapo had special light you had to sit under as they set out to destroy you. Under this red light you had to concentrate on every word you said. You had to have an inner strength to survive. Not everyone had it. At that time, you could have put me under any light—red, green, or whatever—and I wouldn't have broken down. But others did.

When I learned about the Thälmann group, I realized just how smart we had been without even knowing it. Our circle included my husband, a school friend from his childhood in Breslau, and me. The two of them trusted each other implicitly, and they did most of the work. Sometimes they were helped by Paul Putzmann, who was a chauffeur for a man in the SS. Some men are as chatty as women, but not Paul; he knew how to keep a secret. He was also a friend of my husband's and would bring Russians to our home on Ostbahnstrasse.

When my friend Susanna Freund returned from her night shift with stockings and underwear given to her by the soldiers who were returning to the front, we passed them on to the Russians. At our place, they also listened to the radio programs from their homeland. It was all quite dangerous, of course.

During the time that I shared a cell with Hildegard Lehmann in the police headquarters, I noticed what a political dud she was. Perhaps her husband, who was in jail at the same time, was the strong one. I was disappointed that Hildegard Lehmann didn't continue with her political activities.

Not once did I share a cell with a communist who even considered giving me a measly pair of underwear so I could replace the bits of thread I was wearing. Not one! They could exchange their clothes, but I didn't have that luxury. I had always imagined that top-class communists would be sensitive to the needs of their fellow cellmates. They could have, for instance, smuggled out a message in a change of clothes. Because I was a special case, I did not get any clothes or visitors or mail from my husband. I was isolated from everything and treated like the world's worst criminal.

At least the head guard was decent to me. I think it was because I had the necessary discipline. In prison, you could not do what you wanted. You were a prisoner, and at that time I knew how to keep my emotions in check. I also used the guards a bit. I knitted socks and gave other prisoners good advice.

One day Hildegard Lehmann said to me, "My husband is in a cell down below. He's going to be put to death, and I just have to see him one more time. I hope they revoke his death sentence; maybe he'll get fifteen years instead. Anyway, from now on I'm going to be a 'trustee'—a prisoner's assistant." That meant she would deliver meals to the prisoners. Breakfast was ersatz coffee and a slice of bread. "For a woman who was city councillor for the communists," I replied, "you've sunk pretty low. But I'll be glad to have the cell to myself for a bit."

Through her work Hildegard Lehmann could catch some of what was going on. One day she told me that they were going to make me a trustee too. "Heavens, that's going to end in disaster," I said. "But maybe then I'll get to see my husband as well." That same day the head guard approached me when I was alone in the cell. "Prisoner Krause, I have a job for you," she said. "If you breathe a word about it to anyone, you will be sentenced to death. Think it over. We'll tell you more when it's time."

My task was to clean a cell. I wondered what was up because they told me that once I was done, the cell was to remain locked. And I was not to fetch any water for the job; they would do it for me. I figured it had to be something terrible. They told me that one of the prisoners had experienced a bad tooth problem.

I went into the cell. The walls were covered in blood. They had beaten the French woman to death. I knew her only by sight. I had seen her during our short rounds. I had admired her because she was a beautiful woman with a good figure. Other than that I didn't know her at all.

And just what was this beautiful young French woman doing in jail? She was in for high treason and spying. They had beaten her to death the night before because she wouldn't talk. If the Nazis' interrogation methods failed, someone came to wear you down—and if that didn't work, then they beat you. The French woman knew a lot of names, but she refused to give up a single one. A German woman couldn't have done that. You needed so much strength and courage, because what it really came down to was a choice between life or death.

In the morning, Hildegard Lehmann did her assistant's job and I cleaned out the cell. The guards kept the other cells locked while they threw out the bloody water and brought in fresh water. The walls, the bed—everything was covered in blood. I never said a word.

Then Hildegard Lehmann came and asked me what I had done in the other cell. "I noticed you have a screw loose," she accused me.

"And you?" I retorted.

The next day she returned to the cell in tears. "The official in charge spoke to me and then the head guard gave me a dirty look," she said. The officials were always marching around with the police to see if they could curry favour for having arrested someone.

"I told you so," I said.

"I just wanted to see my husband."

She was to be interrogated the next day. "Think carefully about what you're going to say," I warned her. "You told me that your daughter is with the Nazi Girls' Association, the BDM. Just tell them that you worked as a shorthand typist for a big firm. You came home in the evenings totally exhausted because for eight-and-a-half hours you had to concentrate really hard on writing. That's why you can't remember things: you were always so exhausted."

They put Hildegard Lehmann through the wringer. Her husband was sentenced to death. He was guillotined at Münchner Platz, but his grave is in Berlin. I have visited it.

After that, Hildegard Lehmann did something drastic. One night I was restless and fell asleep thinking that something was not right. When I woke up, I saw that she had a rope and was about to hang herself. To bring her back to her senses, I hit her. Did I ever hit her!

"Are you totally crazy? I'm a Jew and I'm with you in this cell. That means they'll think I killed you, you coward! First you're strutting around and blabbering all kinds of shit, and now you want to hang yourself!" I yelled at her some more. Then the crisis ended and everything went back to normal. Hildegard Lehmann lived for a long time after that.

I was moved to the "Jewish Section." There I met Mrs. Hochstein, the last Jew who was to share a cell with me. She had been beaten black and blue. Klemm from the Gestapo had beaten her.

Mrs. Hochstein was from Cologne. I love the way people from Cologne speak, the dialect. She was an elegant and educated woman who was totally spoiled by her husband and the people around her. She came from a rich Jewish home and as a young girl enjoyed every comfort. She had a governess and much more. Her husband was loving and good to her. He treated her as if she were eighteen years old. Her son was a jockey. Her daughter was a dancer and singer who had even performed in front of that son of a bitch Goebbels. The children were half-Jews because her husband was "Aryan."

The Hochsteins had a large racing stable. One night her son, the jockey, saw a light blinking in the stable. He snuck up and saw that one of their own stable boys was cutting the leather straps off the harnesses. At that time, leather was very scarce because it was needed for the war. The police were summoned. The stable boy got his revenge by telling the authorities that Mrs. Hochstein was a Jew. Someone warned the Hochsteins. They fled to Dresden where they were discovered and arrested. The husband was released, but Mrs. Hochstein was beaten nearly to death by Klemm and thrown into a cell with me.

That woman was totally unprepared for life. First I cooled her wounds and then took care of her. Her husband spoiled her. He even brought her a mink coat with a matching hat and elegant shoes. "Are you out of your mind?" I asked her. "How can your husband bring those things in here? When you do the rounds, the others are going to say: 'Look at the Jew, she's all decked out.' And a down quilt! If they take you away, then you'll just be leaving gifts behind for them. Tell your husband to bring your mail but take the other stuff back home with him."

Burned-out ruins of the Old Synagogue of Dresden, after Kristallnacht, November 1938. (Dresdner Hefte 45, no. 14 [1996]: 79.)

Mrs. Hochstein didn't believe me. She believed in goodness. She believed that her husband was fighting for her. But it was useless. You could tell them "I'm an Aryan" ten times over; it didn't help. She had never worked a day in her life. She'd always had servants. So I was her helpmate. I cleaned the cell and told her to eat. I tried to give her courage. As we lived together in the cell, we got to know and like each another. I was younger in years, but I was the one who told her how to behave; it was hard to believe that she was the mother of two children. She was truly grateful. She knew that the moment I was taken away to a camp, she would not be able to survive.

When that day arrived, I found myself in a cell with all the other people who had received their "train tickets" for the transports to Auschwitz, Ravensbrück, and other camps. You had to leave your own cell the day before the transport and spend the night in the communal cell. Instead of beds there were blankets on the floor, so you had to stand or sit.

I approached the duty officer. "You know very well that I'm being sent to a camp," I said, "and that I don't believe in life after death."

"How should I know that," she said.

"Well, it's true," I said, "and someone up above knows it too. I have a request. You and I both know that Mrs. Hochstein isn't going to make it without me. May I spend the last night by her side?"

She looked at me. "I'm not allowed to," she said, "but... okay. I know you won't tell on me. I'll fetch you early in the morning."

And so I spent the night with Mrs. Hochstein. All night long she hung on my neck like a child, and we didn't sleep a wink. She was incapable of taking care of herself. In the morning, I had to return to the communal cell.

After the war, Mr. Hochstein visited me in my place of business. He found me through a search agency. He didn't know that our house on Ostbahnstrasse had been destroyed during the Allied bombing. At one time during my imprisonment with his wife, Mr. Hochstein had taken a secret message to Max in our house on Ostbahnstrasse. Unfortunately, Max had not been home and so he had slipped it under the door with a note saying that I was in the same cell as his wife. When Mr. Hochstein contacted me after the war, he asked me: "How did my wife die? What happened to her?" I had to tell him every word that his wife and I had exchanged.

It troubled me greatly. This man had loved his wife so much and had fought so hard to save her. I tried to console him. "You couldn't do anything more for her," I said. "It was to be expected. She didn't know enough about the real world. Her life had always gone smoothly. She went from a good and loving home into an even more loving marriage. She had no idea what fascism was. I had a very different life. I faced hardships that she never faced, and that's what saved me. I was first jailed right when fascism started up. When they set the synagogues on fire, I knew it was the beginning of the end. I was a child of the back streets and your wife was a queen. Life in jail was beyond her comprehension. That's why she perished like so many others."

Mr. Hochstein loved his wife more than anything in the world. Their children are still alive.

9 In the Women's Concentration Camp, Ravensbrück

No one is willing to say exactly what it was like in a concentration camp. Solidarity? That's just old hat because you only had your own life—you only thought of your own survival. That meant: don't stick out, do your work as best you can with whatever energy you have, and nothing more. Period.

Ravensbrück: Line up!

Auschwitz: Line up!

With a lot of yelling and marching about, we were off. I didn't know where the transport was headed. I just followed my group. We were a large group, and every ten prisoners were under the control of an officer from the *Volkssturm*, the "People's Militia." We had to march in rows of five, so that for every two rows there was one of them. Prisoners who had already tried to escape were in chains. The entire communal cell from Dresden was transported to Bautzen. Then I was sent to a jail in Görlitz on the way to Poland. I saw many more prisons in the months that followed. I was imprisoned in Löbau, in Alexanderplatz and Moabit in Berlin, and in another small prison whose name I don't remember.

The prison in Moabit was tolerable. I had been watching the guards in Berlin for some time. Which one should I approach? I wondered. Which one will do something for me? One guard was ready to let me go if I slept with him, but I only wanted him to mail a letter that I'd written with great difficulty.

In Alexanderplatz prison, I shared a communal cell with some prostitutes. I approached one of them. She was pale but tough as an old nag. "Could you get me a pencil?" I asked. "I also need paper and a stamp." Not long after, she presented me with two envelopes, paper, and stamps. Now is that a buddy, or what? I'll never judge women in that trade. Many of them came from good homes.

I wrote the letters fast. My biggest worry was how to get them mailed. I started checking out the guards. Just when I thought that I'd found a good candidate, he would start yelling and screaming. Still, I had noticed that the guards who tended to yell and were really impulsive weren't so bad after all. One day I said to one of these guards, "I have a letter. I'm being sent to a concentration camp. Could you take it for me?" He looked the other way before responding with a curt "okay." With typical brusqueness, he took the letter and quickly concealed it. That guy wouldn't have hurt a fly. He just pretended to be tough.

I took the second letter into the cattle car with me. My plan was to throw it out of an opening in the train when we passed a mailbox. From inside I could see the mailbox and the postwoman. What I didn't see was the SS man. But then the postwoman snatched up that letter and deposited it in the box. Super! That's how my husband found out that I was being sent to a concentration camp. He had written countless letters requesting that I be pardoned. At least now he would know where I was going.

In those cattle cars, the guards would make out right in front of us. An SS man and an SS woman would choose the best place, spread out, and have sexual intercourse while the rest of us wrestled for a bit of space. I was at the front at first, but it was too crowded so I moved to a corner in the back where I could sit up.

I woke in the night because we had to get out. We had arrived at Ravensbrück. Thank goodness I still had my own clothes on. My husband had given me a tailored coat made of British cloth. He always gave me such wonderful things. He would have given me the stars in the sky if he could have. I used material from the coat to make myself a hat so I didn't freeze. It was only ten degrees in that cattle car.

We had to get out and walk through the night to Ravensbrück concentration camp. Actually, I should have gone to Auschwitz but they said it was full. We stood outside Ravensbrück all night. A train arrived with a large group from Auschwitz. It was at that moment that I first realized what was really going on. These people were completely run down and in rags. They stank, they were dirty, and they had lice. I didn't have lice yet, and I was still in my own clothes. I had wonderful lined boots, a blouse, and a coat. The people from Auschwitz had nothing.

Johanna's concentration camp number with the red triangle indicating "political prisoner." (Ravensbrück Concentration Camp Memorial Museum.)

So we stood the whole night in front of the camp. In the morning, half frozen, we entered the camp. I could tell what was coming from the way the SS were yelling at us. We were separated into groups. There were the political prisoners, the communists, and so on. We were inspected and pushed around. "You have such a nice overcoat," a prisoner said to me. "They're going to take it from you and put a white stripe on it, and that's for the Kapo. It'd be stolen anyway." Everything was stolen. I had a few nice things with me in prison—a ring, a bracelet, and a Montblanc pen case— but they had always been returned to me.

After some time, the overseer received my file. "Come here!" she said harshly. "Why are you here?"

"I insulted the Führer," I answered, referring to my arrest in 1933.

"This Jewish pig insulted the Führer! Look at this swine! Insulting our Führer! Heil Hitler! Heil Hitler!" She belted me on the ear with such force that I flew into a corner.

I was stripped and forced to take an ice-cold shower. The overseer was still screaming. She was working herself into a frenzy, a real ecstasy. In the end, she was so carried away by her rage that she gave me the red triangle— the political triangle—and forgot to give me the yellow star for Jews. That's how I became a political prisoner. That saved me. Otherwise I wouldn't be alive today.

The red triangle was sewn onto my prison clothes. I later gave my triangle to the people running the museum at Ravensbrück.

The prisoners coming from Auschwitz thought that things would be different at Ravensbrück. They were wrong. Day and night you could smell burning flesh. Our heads were shaved and soon we were full of lice just like them. The Polish prisoners wouldn't let us go to the wash basins. They pushed us aside because, after all, the Germans had caused all the misery they found themselves in. There were prisoners from around the world in the camp. There must have been twenty or more different countries represented—and all of them were there because of the Germans. That's why the other prisoners hated the German prisoners so much.

The sliver of soap they gave us was stolen. I couldn't imagine that everyone would steal like that. In the concentration camp, everyone filched. My thick socks, my wooden clogs that we had been given on arrival ... gone when I woke one morning. When I asked where my things were, everyone just laughed. So during the roll call, I had to stand barefoot outside in the cold. The roll call lasted at least two hours, and if someone had tried to escape it could go on all night long as they counted and counted and counted. I didn't want to end up going to roll call naked, so, like the others, I slept in my clothes and I "acquired" another pair of clogs. In the camps, everything got pilfered. That's how it worked.

And then there was the food. What little we had to eat we tried to beat out of one another. They would give us a lousy little pot with a few ounces of soup. For months we ate potato peels, rutabaga, and beetroot. The prisoners who pushed their way to the front got the thick part of the soup. It all boiled down to me, myself, and I; just like in a herd of animals, the survival of the fittest. For breakfast we got two slices of bread and a bit of ersatz coffee. That was the prisoners' diet. In fact, there were different kitchens—one for the prisoners and one for the SS. The communist prisoners worked in the kitchen.

Nowadays you hear all the former political prisoners say they were heroes. But they worked in the kitchen or in the woodworking shop. Those of us without set duties were stuck with the dirty work. Dirty work was the worst work of all. You had to work in the toilet barracks emptying the overflowing pails of shit. Even though it was cold the shit stank terribly, and then you stank too because you could barely wash yourself.

I had to carry heavy rocks up a hill, right to the top, and then make it back down again. You had to watch out that a rock didn't fall on you. At the bottom of the hill stood the SS, and God help you if you lent a hand to someone who was lying there and couldn't go on; then you got shot in the back of the neck or they'd set the dogs on you—dogs trained to go for the throat. They called this work idiots' work. And then there were prisoners who had to load the corpses onto the handcarts.

Others had to do work that no one really knew about. For such work they used women who had the skull and crossbones marked on their files; women like me. They used us because we were to be exterminated anyway. Actually, it was work I was glad to do because it was done outside the camp and we were not harassed and bullied. Once a week, we were marched into the forest. A path through the woods led to a ditch with holes. To the left stood the gas truck. To the right and left of the path were the clothes and other belongings of the dead people who had been thrown out of the gas truck. The dead people were gone but you could tell from the belongings where they came from: France, Belgium, Poland, or Russia. Children and adults from the country or the city—all this you could see by the things left behind.

We had to sort these things because there were no more clothes for prisoners in the camp. They gave us the private clothes with a big white cross painted on the back and a number sewn on. After we had sorted everything, they frisked us. One time I managed to steal a little paring knife with the word "France" engraved on it. I still have that knife today. They tried to take it away from me a couple of times, but I hid it in my bosom. A knife like that was worth its weight in gold.

So that was the work that was done by the people who were slated for extermination. There were to be no witnesses. That was the work that no one knows about.

In the camp, there was a room called the idiots' room. The prisoners who sniggered and laughed about the women in that room couldn't hold a candle to them. The women in there were highly educated; they could speak many languages. During the transport, they would sit in a corner reading English books. They were intelligent women, intellectuals. The SS couldn't hold a candle to them either.

Most of these women went insane. They couldn't imagine what would happen to them in the idiots' room. They were beautiful women from good homes, and they were all driven crazy. At night, when the SS were drunk, they came and "amused" themselves with these women.

There was a brothel in Ravensbrück. They only took the good-looking women. The young Jewish women were particular favourites because they looked so good with their hair done up. But the camp commanders wanted to exterminate all the Jewish women, and that's what happened. Today they say people helped the Jews, but I never saw any of these women again.

In the concentration camp, I was reserved. I did not speak a word to anyone. If a prisoner wanted something from me, I ignored her. Some of them were so brutal. I can't even describe it. Elbowing, pilfering, defending yourself, and steering clear of the beasts—you had to learn all that. Being cautious, I set up a system for myself. I analyzed things and calculated odds—anything in the world that might help me survive.

I got to know a Jewish woman in the neighbouring barrack. She was a good fifteen years younger than me, and very attractive. She had the top bunk, and we would chat and exchange information there. She gave me many tips. Then she had to rush off to work. When the overseer wasn't looking, I would sneak off the bunk and back into my barrack. I don't know if the woman survived.

In the evenings, if I had the presence of mind, I would lie in bed and think about my life. I would look up at the four-tier bunks and see all the phlegm and pus and discharge and other stuff that ran down the bedpost. There were lice everywhere.

For weeks on end we didn't have even a tiny puddle of water to wash in. We stank. We were sick. We had dysentery and typhoid fever. We were four to a bunk, lying there like in a nest. The women in the upper bunks had to lie on their sides, some of them pregnant or so sick that everything was a torture. Then down came the pus. You'd be lying there and this stuff would drip onto your face. Or there would be stinky feet in your face because we had to lie at impossible angles in order to fit on the bed. Those were the conditions we lived under. You can't even describe them really. No soldier lived like that. Soldiers lay in ditches, but they got their food and were treated like human beings. We were no longer human.

In our barrack there was one exception to this, and that was a professional hairdresser named Edith Schramann. She cut the hair of the SS. This earned her special privileges; she had her own locker and she smelled of perfume. The SS didn't want to get any lice from her, so Edith Schramann became the great lady who could spit down on us. We were the dirty pigs who stank to high heaven.

One day I was walking along the main camp street when I came upon a huge pile of rutabagas in front of a kitchen. Nearly crazed with hunger, I stole one. They were frozen together, and I almost broke my hand trying to get it. Today I'm picky about food, but that wasn't an option in the camps: we would have been long dead if we'd been fussy about dirt. Anyway, I was caught sharing my rutabaga and ended up in the punishment barracks. In those cells, there was one long hall. The windows were nailed shut so that light could enter only through a slit. There was shit everywhere. The people in there had lost their senses. There was a crazy *Blockova*. This overseer beat us and then everyone beat up on everyone else. An old person would never have survived. But I was still young and in my prime, and I knew how to avoid them all.

I stayed in the punishment barracks for at least eight weeks. You were treated like the lowest animal there. At some point, I was ordered to appear before the commander and beaten twenty times on the back and legs. Thankfully someone advised me beforehand to keep my mouth shut during the beating: "If you moan out loud, they start again until you're dead. So just don't think of anything—and don't count." I got out of there alive, but to survive that beating ... and how I looked! You couldn't go to the sick bay if you were a Jew; that would have meant immediate death. Early the next morning, I was in agony when roll call tore me out of my bunk. I was transferred to another barrack.

If friendship is possible in a concentration camp, I didn't experience it. Maybe some women helped others, offered a supporting hand while working, but it never happened to me. From what I observed, everyone was a traitor. No one can tell me there was goodness there. It was like living among animals. The stronger ones yanked the weaker ones out of their bunks and kicked them. We fought like cats and dogs over the tiniest scrap of food.

A few years ago, I attended a meeting at Ravensbrück. "Wasn't there anyone you were close to?" a woman asked me. "Everyone needs love."

"Good lord," I replied, "love was the first thing to perish!"

You didn't know who the woman next to you really was. You survived by not speaking, not drawing attention to yourself, not fighting with anyone, and not making friends.

On the night that Dresden was bombed, we acted as if something wonderful had happened. We cried tears of joy and shouted, "It's the end! It's the end!" We celebrated. We didn't think of the people who lost all their possessions. I've lost everything five times in my life. You can always replace the material stuff. But your life—that you can't replace.

Postcard from Max Krause to Johanna indicating that he had survived the bombing of Dresden in February 1945. (Estate of Johanna Krause.) *Translation: Side 1 (top)*—Postmark: Sebnitz, Saxony, Feb. 17, 1945 | **Urgent Message** | To: Mrs. Johanna Krause | Born: Oct. 23, 1907, Dresden | Address: Ravensbrück | Post office Fürstenberg (Mecklenburg); *Side 2 (above)*—**Sign of Life from**: Krause, Max | From: Dresden A, 24 Ostbahnstrasse | Date: Feb. 17, 1945 (Maximum 10 words allowed) | At this point in Sebnitz, Mandaner Str. 26 | Greetings and kisses, Max.

For four days in a row, I had given a comrade my food ration and so I had nothing in my stomach. I was like a zombie. We were all zombies in the concentration camp. I couldn't eat anymore. I had dysentery and typhoid fever; nothing but blood ran out of me. I wanted to die.

Then a miracle happened. An SS woman approached me. "Are you Johanna Krause?" she asked. "Are you from Dresden?"

"Yes, yes," I answered.

She handed me a postcard. A postcard from my husband! I hadn't heard a word from him in all this time, and suddenly he had written from Sebnitz. When this card arrived, I thought: You must live. Your husband has written you. He needs you. It was as if the sun were shining after a long rain. That card gave me the strength I needed for the death march. Strange, very strange—that card, that one and only card; I kept it in the pocket near my heart.

10 The Death March

Max's card inspired me so much that I approached the woman I had given my food ration to and asked her to give me some of my food back. "I have a new will to live," I told her, "and I'm ready to go on the march." She didn't return the food without a fight. "Breathe your last, you Jewish pig," she said to me.

In February 1945, we were packed into two large buses and transferred from Ravensbrück to Rechlin. Rechlin was not an extermination camp. It was originally a testing centre for the Luftwaffe. Things were a bit better there. The food wasn't so bad, and instead of straw I got to sleep on a mattress; just that improvement was wonderful. But even here, there were curious goings-on. For example, the Jewish leader of the barrack had an affair with the commander. I have no right to judge her for entering into such a liaison. Maybe she wanted to save her own life. Or maybe the affair gave her some sense of control.

One day the commander ordered us all together and made a "great" speech. He informed us that we would be transformed into "proper National Socialists." "You know that I have always stood by you," he added, giving the French woman next to him a jab. "It's the end. I promise you that. It's coming to an end."

Despite his assurances, we were taken back to Ravensbrück after only a few weeks. For the next two weeks, we stayed in barrack 32 while Pflaum, the work unit supervisor, organized a large transport. I knew Pflaum by sight. He was good-looking. God made some of the Nazis good-looking, but that didn't mean a thing—on the inside they were poison.

Naturally, there was no personal contact. We were filthy and crawling with lice, and we stank. We had lovely pet names like hussy, piece of shit, and so on. Pflaum was a really dreadful character. He sent women to their deaths. There had been one last transport to Auschwitz. Two people—myself and a French woman—were removed from that transport. To this day I don't know why.

Then Pflaum put together an even bigger transport. We walked to the village of Ravensbrück, which today is called Fürstenberg. Then we were taken in cattle cars from Dresden to Karlsbad in Czechoslovakia. The trains were bombed throughout the journey. From the wrecked trains the soldiers retrieved dog meat and bones, which had been intended for the military, and threw them on the ground. Our prisoners chewed on the bones and meat like animals. I didn't touch the stuff myself. Not me. Like an old cow, I filled my stomach with sorrel; it grows like grass, and I remembered it from my childhood.

In Karlsbad, we set out on foot to the Neurolau concentration camp. In Neurolau, there was that certain stench in the air too. A couple of days after our arrival, a woman said, "Come with me." She took me to a large room. In that room, lying next to each other, were the bodies of the women from the transport. They had been done in by that dog meat. They had all died a wretched death. One of the dead was the woman I had nearly given my food ration to, the woman who had told me to breathe my last.

You don't have to be strictly religious or orthodox to believe that there's something like justice in this world. What is it? God? Or angels maybe? Whatever it is, a year later I rejoined the Jewish community because all the things I had gone through restored my faith.

One night in March, in just half an hour, the entire Neurolau camp was evacuated. There were over a thousand prisoners from every possible country. We were marched to Karlsbad, guarded by a contingent of SS men and women as well as a pack of bloodhounds. In Karlsbad we were piled into cattle cars and taken to Petschau, Egerland. The train tracks there had been damaged by the bombing, and the American soldiers were closing in. I could see it all coming to an end. We were supposed to march to Dachau because the gas ovens there were said to be still functioning.

In the Bohemian forest, we couldn't go on because we were surrounded by the Red Army on one side and the Americans on the other. The guards were getting more and more fearful by the minute, and they chased us willy-nilly through the forest. At night, many of our group tried to escape into the bushes. Most of them were bitten to death by the dogs, or shot or fatally beaten by the SS. Those women who couldn't keep up the pace and fell behind were struck with the butts of SS guns.

Only a few of us made it to Kladrau, where they hid us in a barn. I had a raging fever. I also had typhoid and dysentery. I had stopped having bowel movements; only blood came out. In that state, you can't eat anymore but you constantly have to relieve yourself. Even in my delirium, I heard the SS people talking among themselves about how they were surrounded by Americans. Too feverish to consider the consequences, I crept out of the barn and saw the SS standing there. As they kept discussing things, I went around to the back of the barn. I squatted and the blood came flowing out.

Then I heard shooting.

After a while, it was totally quiet. I lay there behind the barn. Suddenly, breaking the silence, two foreign women came toward me. I wasn't even shocked. I just stood up and said, "Okay, you can shoot me too."

"Put your hands down," one of them replied. "Don't you see who we are?"

I looked at them properly and saw that they were wearing the red triangles, with "R" for Russia and "P" for Poland. We all had these triangles. In the silence that followed, we mustered the courage to crawl out of our hiding place and enter the barn. There we saw the rest of our group lying every which way; they had been shot to death.

On our last reserves of strength, we set out. Somewhere between Kladrau and Mühlhöfen, I fell to the ground. I was totally spent. My comrades were too weak to drag me with them.

In Mühlhöfen, in a cow barn, I came to my senses. A farmer had picked me up from the side of the road and brought me there. The local priest was called to give me the last rites. I was not far from death when children came running into the barn.

"Father, father!" they cried out.

"What's going on?"

"You have to come right away to the town hall. The Americans have just marched into town!"

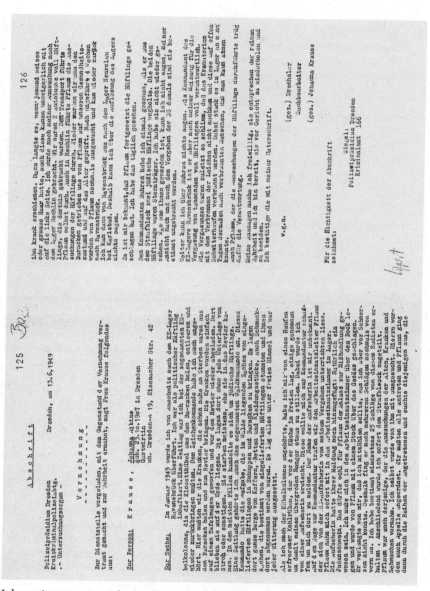

Johanna's statement, submitted on June 13, 1949, in the court case against Pflaum, the work unit supervisor at Ravensbrück. (Estate of Johanna Krause.) *Translation opposite.*

Copy

Police Headquarters, Dresden   Dresden, June 13, 1949
Criminal Investigation Department
Committee of Inquiry

Hearing

Having been requested to appear, and having been informed of the subject under
investigation, and having been admonished to tell the truth, Mrs. Krause made the
following statement:

Identity: K r a u s e, Johanna Albine
           Born Oct. 23, 1907 in Dresden
           Restaurant Owner
           Address: Dresden 19, Eisenacher Str. 42

The case: In January 1945, I was transported to Ravensbrück concentration camp.
          I was incarcerated as a political prisoner. For a while, I was in the so-
called "cubicle work unit," which fetched the toilet pails from the barracks, then emptied and returned them. I also was part of the "corpse work unit."
This work required us to transport sick and half-dead women from the barracks to
the sick bay. The sick were simply thrown onto a flat cart and dumped in front of
the sick bay. They just lay there on the ground. They lay there without a bit of straw
under them or anything. Most of them died before being admitted to the sick bay.
In most cases, they were Jewish prisoners. For a while, I was part of the so-called
"forest work unit." This work unit had to go to the forest and retrieve the belongings of prisoners. We had to put the things in storehouses and in the barracks.
There were mountains of suitcases, bedclothes, and clothes, as well as jewellery,
which undoubtedly had been taken from the prisoners. The things lay exposed to
the elements under the open sky.

When I was part of the cubicle work unit, I took a few rutabaga from a pile of
frozen ones in front of the kitchen. I needed to do something for my terrible
hunger. I was caught by a guard who wanted to take me to headquarters to register
my crime. I don't know the name of that female guard. On the way, we met the
work unit supervisor, Pflaum. The guard told him what I had done. Pflaum took me
immediately to his office in the camp. The guard noted in her report: "Of course,
it's a Jewish pig." That must have been the reason Pflaum abused me. In his office, I
had to bend over the beating table and I was beaten on the backside. He demanded
that I count with him, which I could not do because of the pain. So he started from
zero again and beat me again. I received at least twenty-five lashes from that sadist.
From there I was taken directly to the punishment cell. Pflaum was also the one
who made selections among the old, the sick, and the weak. I was selected by him
one time. A roll call was ordered. We all had to appear and Pflaum went up and
down the rows and chose those who appeared to him to be sick. If you had white or
grey hair, that was enough to be selected to go to the left. After my selection, I was
taken to the Rechlin camp. The prisoners taken to Rechlin filled two buses. Pflaum
himself organized the transport. Once again, we were driven from our barracks by

Pflaum and checked for the state of our health or age. After about four weeks, we were selected once more by Pflaum and transported back to Ravensbrück.

I was taken from Ravensbrück to the Neurolau bei Karlsbad. Therefore, I can make no statement about the dissolution of the Ravensbrück camp.

I know that Pflaum continually beat prisoners. I saw this on a daily basis.

I saw the Commander Suhren take two Jewish prisoners out of the punishment cell one time. Both prisoners wore the yellow star. I never saw them again. I don't know what happened to them. In my opinion—and considering how the SS acted in general—I would say they were definitely killed.

I cannot say more about Suhren. As commander of the Ravensbrück concentration camp, he is in my opinion fully responsible for the gassing of thousands of prisoners. The gassings were so bad at the end that the crematoriums could not keep up with burning the corpses so they were often burned on pyres. It stunk so badly from burning human flesh that one could hardly breathe. Pflaum, who selected the prisoners, is also responsible for that.

I have made these statements voluntarily; the statements are the whole truth. I am prepared to repeat these statements in court under oath.

I confirm the authenticity of my signature.

Signed: Drechsler
Clerk
Signed: Johanna Krause

Attesting to the authenticity of this protocol:

Seal of the police HQ of Dresden
Office of Criminal Investigation 166

11 After Liberation

The American soldiers who occupied the village took me to a hospital in Miess where I recovered from my phlegmon, dysentery, and typhoid fever. I was well treated there.

One day an American soldier approached me. "You have to leave now, okay? We're taking you to Plan bei Marienbad."

"I know all the Germans have to leave, but I'm not German," I replied. "I'm Hungarian."

"You're married to a German, and so you're German. Besides, you're much better now and Plan has some excellent nurses; all they do is pray and heal."

So, in May 1945 I became an in-patient in the Sankta Anna hospital in Plan bei Marienbad. In Plan there were former *Wehrmacht* medical captains who had to take an oath to keep us alive. They really did everything they could to fulfill that pledge. As well as myself there were other prisoners who had been picked up along the way, but I never saw anyone from my transport again.

I ended up in surgery because during the death march I had fallen behind and been hit on the back of the head with a rifle butt. The blood had flowed, and the lice had gotten in there to suck the blood. The nurses cleaned the wound. The skin on my neck was full of wrinkles and the dirt had penetrated the skin. I stank really badly until they treated me with oil; it took them eight weeks to get me really clean.

The head doctor, Dr. Wilhelm Tröstenberg, treated us very well. There was a Professor Barton who took a particular interest in me. He really helped me out one time. We were in the small city of Plan (a farming community) looking for clothes for me to wear, but the three shops we visited didn't want to give me anything. At one point, Professor Barton took out his gun and said, "That's it, I'll give you ten minutes to check your inventory. If you don't give this woman what she needs, we'll find it ourselves." That's how I ended up with some underwear and a shirt. I didn't need a bra because there was nothing left—gone, as if they had withered away in the wind. Terrible!

They were all very sweet to me in the hospital. One day I went to the head nurse and asked, "Do you think it's possible for me to go to the city hall? I have nothing to wear and I want to change so I can have my old clothes deloused." The nurse gave me a pair of her own pants; they were embroidered and had a slit in the side that ran the length of the leg. I was wearing those pants and a striped hospital shirt when I went to city hall. By that time there were new people in control—the communists. I asked if it would be possible to get a shirt, underwear, a dress, or some money. The man I spoke with said no. What he meant was that these things were for his people; there wasn't enough to go around.

As I was leaving, I almost collided with a tall officer—an American with epaulettes on his uniform. He approached me and spoke a few words. I was afraid he wanted to arrest me, but he said he only wanted to help. "Are you Hebraic?" he asked. I nodded. "Then as long as I am in the occupying forces here," he continued, "you are going to be taken care of." He later helped me get a room. But first I had to return to the hospital to recover from TB. I lay there every night as if I had wet the bed. I sweated so much that my shirts were soaking wet. I sweated the TB out of my lungs until I healed.

One day the tall American came to me. "I'm going to pick you up on Friday," he said. "I'll speak to the head nurse about it." Now they're going to lock you up, I thought, and he just won't tell you. But that wasn't the case. After everything I'd been through, I didn't trust a soul … and that mistrust has never left me. Anyway, he picked me up on Friday and took me to a school. There were many Americans there. It was Shabbos. I had no idea there were so many Jewish-American soldiers. There were some regular soldiers, but many of them were officers of various ranks. When I entered, they all called out "rise!" Then they bowed and sat me down in the middle. I was wearing those pants with the slit up the side, and they hooted at that as I sat there, right in the middle.

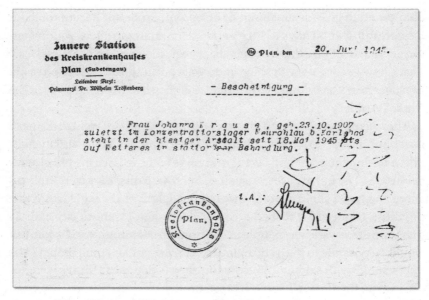

Document issued by hospital in Plan, Czechoslovakia, where Johanna was treated after the death march. (Estate of Johanna Krause.) *Translation:* Confirmation—Mrs. Johanna Krause, born Oct. 23, 1907, was recently in the Neurohlau bei Karlsbad concentration camp. She has been in the above-named hospital since May 18, 1945, and will remain here for in-patient treatment until further developments.

The service began. They gave me a little green prayer book in English. At the end of it all they gave me a huge package of stuff. I thought of asking them for money instead because I didn't need all those things. But the American said that I would be provided for and that I should be patient; he vowed to help me. I kept the vitamins for myself and gave the rest of the things to the nurses. I had enough to eat at the hospital. The nurses and the head nurse were impressed with the American. But then he had to leave. I was alone once again, and all of a sudden the nurses stopped being so kind.

After I was discharged, I left the hospital and settled in the city of Plan. Before leaving, the tall American had had found me a room in a house because he had great plans for me. I could have had a good life. Everything I went through later on could have been avoided. It was all because the Russian and American soldiers couldn't agree if the war should continue or not. On top of that, cities and towns were being swapped between the two powers; I was under American occupation at first. I had a room that was paid for but no food. Sometimes one of the Americans would bring me something, but it was not regular support.

One day while looking out of my window I saw a young woman at the train station. Her mama, as I later discovered, ran a small business. I asked the woman why there were so many Americans going in and out of her house. "I iron their clothes," she said. The Americans were very clean and well groomed. They had those olive green jackets and pants with a crease that ran the entire length of the leg and had to be pressed accurately.

"Would it be possible for me to help you with your housework?" I asked the woman. "I can't do any farm work because I'm a city girl, but I can knit, mend, clean, and do needlework. I won't steal from you; I own nothing and will steal nothing. In exchange you give me my meals and two free hours a day after I've served the food and done the washing up. I want to go into the village every day and see if I can find a Jewish man or woman who has returned. Also, I don't have a kronen or a dollar to my name, so I'd be grateful if I could do the ironing for a couple of your Americans."

The farm woman did indeed take me in. But one fine day as the devil would have it—and with me there was always something up—this farmer woman said to me, "A relative of mine is visiting. He's working in the field, so you need to cook an extra meal." When I offered to deliver it as well, she said, "No, no. Just fill up this pot. I'll take it to him myself."

A few days later, an American policeman came to the farm. "Haven't you had enough?" he asked me.

"What do you mean?"

"Preparing meals for an SS man!"

"Me? Where did you get that idea, for heaven's sake!"

"Up there in the field we found a man with SS symbols tattooed on his arm."

I apologized and told him the whole story. I couldn't calm down. They picked the man up, and I just kept on working.

Then I started going into the village every day, and soon the entire village knew me. "That's the little one who's looking for a Jewish man or woman," they would say. "My God, we only have farming here. Was she was in a camp? Maybe that's what makes her so strange. You never know. Some people had it bad."

Every day that God gave me, for a quarter of a year, I walked around asking people.

"No, we never had any Jews here!"

By this time everyone was laughing and thinking, what's up with this woman, because I had approached them over and over again. Then one day a woman stopped her car and asked me to get in.

"Tell me, who are you actually looking for?"

"A Jewish man or a Jewish woman," I answered.

"I have some information," she said.

"I can't get into the car with you," I said. "I don't even know you."

"But I know you," the lady said. "You have spoken to me before but you've forgotten." I really had forgotten because I had spoken to so many people.

"There was a bakery here," the lady continued. "It belonged to a family with a daughter. She wasn't Jewish—she was blond and had long braids. But she married a Jewish man in Prague and still lives in Prague. As soon as this woman's husband arrives, I'll come to your place and pick you up. But please, please, stay at home now, and don't go around asking about this anymore."

Finally, I had a lead.

Some weeks later, the woman in the car came to me and said, "Mr. Löbel is here now." We drove to his house. First we checked out the bakery. The Germans had been driven out, of course, and the Czechs had taken it over. Only those Germans who married Czechs and became Czech citizens were allowed to stay.

Mr. Löbel owned the bakery. He was single by then. Because he had been in Auschwitz and a number of other concentration camps, the belongings of his wife's parents—including the cake shop and the apartment— had been given to him. Otherwise everything would have gone to the state.

After a while, Mr. Löbel arrived in his truck. He had been in a small accident and had injured his leg. He went straight to bed and then called out, "Send the Jew in!" I went to his bedside. "My God, are you ever shy," he remarked. "They've robbed you of your senses. You're a free person now."

"I'm not free," I protested. "I have no money. I have nothing but my things from the concentration camp. After I left the camp, a doctor gave

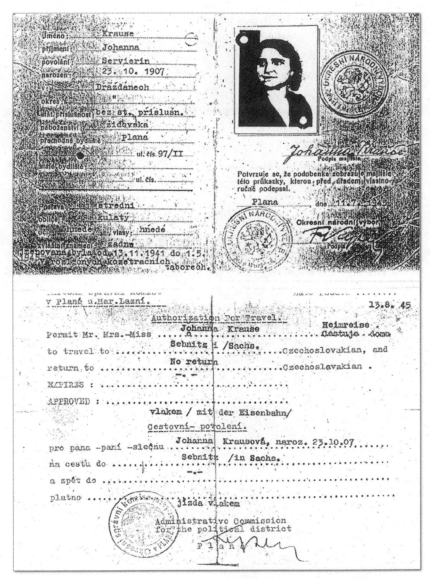

Johanna's authorization-for-travel pass (issued in Plana, Czechoslovakia), which allowed her to return to Sebnitz (near Dresden), where she had last had word from Max. (Estate of Johanna Krause.)

me a document saying I was treated in Miess and then in Plan. But I have no passport and I don't get along with the people here. I can't speak any Czech."

"That's not an obstacle," he said. "I speak five languages. I'll get your repatriation pass; it's a Czech pass in four languages. I'll get you all the documents you need. Otherwise you'll never get away from here, and obviously you can't stay."

"You don't understand," I countered. "Every second day I get an offer from the Americans to go to a good household in Sweden, Denmark, or Holland. I could even go to America or Munich if I wanted."

I conferred with Mr. Löbel for a long time, and in the end I turned down the Americans' offer. "Why do you want to go back to Dresden?" the captain asked. "You're a Jew—the Russians are going to put you in jail again."

"I can't leave," I answered. "My husband lost his career. He was beaten by the Nazis. He did it all for me. I would feel like a swine if I abandoned him now. I just can't do it. And it's peace now, isn't it? Fascism is over."

"Mark my words," the captain said as we parted.

I think of him every day, because things turned out exactly as he predicted.

12 The Eisenacher Hof

The repatriation pass was my guardian angel. With the help of that document, I returned to Dresden in October 1945. I went immediately to Ostbahnstrasse and saw that our house had been totally destroyed in the bombing.

Where was Max? I asked around and discovered that he had hidden from the Gestapo in the Erzgebirge. He had returned to Dresden following the Red Army's arrival there in June 1945. At last we were reunited, but our joy was short-lived. My husband was skin and bones, and he was deathly ill with TB again. He suffered lung problems for the rest of his life. I wasn't totally well myself. I didn't have any broken bones, but I often passed out—just like that—on the street. But Max was sicker than I was. After he was discharged from the hospital, I nursed him back to health.

As a result of the bombing, we lost everything. Max's paintings, which had been stored in a barn, disappeared; the frames were used for firewood. Later Max used my descriptions to create drawings of scenes in the camps. Today one of those drawings is housed in the Holocaust Memorial Museum in Washington. The museum people used the drawing on the cover of their catalogue. They invited me to visit the museum, but by then I could no longer travel alone.

I learned that I had been declared dead for a year. People were shocked but delighted to see me. They strewed my way with flowers. "Don't forget the Communist Party, Johanna!" they said. I found work with the People's Solidarity Association because someone suggested that it would be good for me to become more social. Because I had just returned from a concentration camp, I met with some success at first. Then they dropped me like a rock. Like someone doing penance, I carried out all the shit work,

Ostbahnstrasse, where Johanna and Max had their studio apartment, as it looked after the bombing of Dresden on February 13–14, 1945. (Saxon State and University Library Dresden, German Photothek #Ps 34. Photo by Richard Peter Sr.)

hacking bricks back into shape. It was madness. Our hours were registered on a time sheet, and they'd give us a silver pin for, say, twenty-five hours. I must have been off my rocker to do all that, but I wanted to get back to work and we needed to eat. I couldn't let Max and myself just drop dead.

Anyway, I would hammer those bricks back into shape for hours on end and return home totally filthy. I did everything I could to get people to take me seriously; in other words, I humiliated myself. But I just wanted to be treated like a human being again.

I was living in Blasewitz and asking myself why I wasn't doing something else when the Communist Party made me an offer. "You've worked so long in the restaurant business," they said. "The party needs a restaurant that can be used as a meeting place by comrades who are being trained for a move to Berlin." (In those days, many comrades underwent training in the party school in Dresden before going to Berlin.) They promised me food, coal, potatoes, a telephone—everything that was in short supply at the time.

Johanna, 1945. (Estate of Johanna Krause.)

I approached my former boss, Else Bagehorn, who lived nearby. "Else, let's run the place together. Let's go see it."

The Eisenacher Hof was in Dresden-Striesen, Behrischstrasse 9. It had been a very fascist quarter with swastikas on every house. Across the street was the former Nazi headquarters and to the right their meeting place, the Iron Mead. My interest in the restaurant instantly waned when I saw all that. But then Else said to me, "If you want your husband to get well, you better take the place because only then can you make sure you have enough food for him."

In the beginning, of course, the Eisenacher Hof was a pile of rubble. The windows were broken. The wind played music until the place rattled. Everything inside was broken. It took us until May 1946 to fix it all up. The craftsmen I hired—locksmiths, carpenters, people to lay the floors—were paid for by the state. They were efficient and honest and did excellent work.

The entire time I was down on my knees cleaning. I bought the dishes for the kitchen and had Meissen tiles installed. Many of these expenses were out of pocket, and so I went into debt. Because I'd worked for her, Else Bagehorn lent me money. There was no contract; she trusted me. In the end, I paid back every cent. The previous landlord had to pay his own debts, but he did so only after terrible fights. It was a very difficult time.

The Eisenacher Hof on Behrischstrasse, circa 1950. Max is standing to the left of the front entrance. (Estate of Johanna Krause.)

The beautiful soft red curtains Max bought were the finishing touch. There was no real curtain material at the time so we used red dress fabric instead. The place looked fantastic, more like an artist's café than a bar; there was a back room, a clubroom, and a large main room where most of the customers sat. The Eisenacher Hof was a big success.

I had received a sack of peas and a sack of flour. With these special provisions, I could prepare a meal for between thirty and forty cents. When Max returned from hospital, still not completely healthy, he put himself in charge of the cooking. He went to the local food co-op store and bought things that he could use to make aspic. We made tons of aspic.

If I had too many customers up front, Else came and helped me out, without pay. We also had two hard-working country girls; they didn't get tips in those days, but they could eat their fill. We worked twelve or fourteen hours a day starting early in the morning. We worked very hard, and that's how we were able to pay back the money we had borrowed from Else.

Johanna (*second from right*) and Max with their dachshund Wuschel and guests in the Eisenacher Hof, circa 1950. (Estate of Johanna Krause.)

Else was wonderful! It was only natural that she helped me out. For five years, day after day, we had worked side by side and so we knew each other well. On top of that she trusted me, which was gratifying.

I ran the Eisenacher Hof for thirteen years. The early years were fantastic. There was still the old police station in the neighbourhood. Many of the police were old social democrats who would hold their social evenings at our place. They would sing songs they had written about everything under the sun, including their police comrades and us. One of their songs began with the line, "Hallelujah, Max and Johanna!"; this always took the mickey out of us. It was a lovely time and we had a wonderful home above the restaurant. If we had any problems, we simply called the men from the police station, and they'd show up in the blink of an eye to help. I can't say enough good things about those men.

But then the police station was moved. It was replaced by the Sector Control Police, who controlled an entire zone and reported back to the Stasi (the secret service). The man in our sector was named Heller. I didn't know him personally, but I had a strange feeling about him.

I approached a man named Silberberg from the Jewish community. "Do you know a man called Heller? I heard that he was in control of the Jews in Lodz. I don't know if that's true, but there's something about him I don't like."

"I'll find out for you. I have many Polish friends, and they might know something." Mr. Silberberg asked around and found out that the man had worked under the name "Kraklau." He was Polish and had been with the SA or the SS. He had good reason to have a guilty conscience.

Heller and I did not get along. One time when he was drunk, he complained to Mr. Silberberg that he hadn't been promoted to officer "because of that Krause couple." Obviously, the higher-ups in the party had figured out who this man was and were covering for him and others like him. From that time on, we no longer had any help at our place.

But in those first years when the police station was nearby, people were thankful to have a place like ours. I cooked for two hundred people a day. I could have cooked for six hundred! As well as policemen, my customers included party members and comrades who went on to the cadre school in Berlin. For awhile too I had people from some sort of religious association, and choir singers from the Holy Cross Church. My favourite customers were the mountain climbers. They are special people—honest and intensely loyal to one another. If the place was full, I didn't even have to write down their orders; they would fetch their own food.

We renovated a small, charming artists' room. It was reserved for special customers like dancers from the Palucca School. Dancers from the state theatre came too because word got around that I had an electric piano. It was a first-class piano (a Wolfram), black with a gold frame. I had it converted into a regular piano. It was especially cherished by the mountain climbers because they loved to sing their mountain-climbing songs. The news spread and that special class of people—the artists—came to us. The regular guests frowned on them because they understood nothing of the life of an artist; they thought artists were people of ill repute. But with the artists there was dancing and a spirited atmosphere.

One day Mr. Böhme from the state theatre stopped by just as Roberta Förster-Frohberger was singing. He was married but had his girlfriend on his arm. That's how artists are. "My God, that's a trained voice!" he exclaimed. "I know one when I hear one." Then he saw my piano and started to sing along. As an employee of the state theatre, he wasn't technically allowed to. But he did it anyway.

Then I bought an accordion, which appealed to the other type of customer. We hired two friends. One sang while the other played. They had good voices too. Neither wanted any money for it. They were fed and could have a drink, and they were satisfied with that. They played and their crowd came along.

During this time, Roberta Förster-Frohberger became my friend. It was in the stars. Sometimes at the start of a friendship you have a feeling—it just has to happen. She was a wonderful woman with a unique voice; when she sang, it sent shivers down your spine. It still hurts me to think about how she went downhill—but that was later.

Roberta came from a funny family. At that time, she lived with her mother and her daughter Bärbel. Her husband, an officer cadet, had been killed in the war. Her daughter got an education and eventually married; in later years, she sometimes wrote to me and helped me out. Roberta's brother was shot here in Dresden because he had been a Nazi, the idiot. Her father had served as an officer under the emperor. Her mother was elegant and refined, like a baroness. Roberta herself was an artist through and through. She lived in a huge apartment and schooled her students in both classical and popular songs. She trained a very famous singer, but on weekends she made music herself.

She could sing and speak Russian perfectly, so during the occupation the Russians would get her to sing for them. The Russians, especially the officers, liked to get her drunk on vodka before she sang. Gulp, gulp—down the gullet. That's how it all started. She was always falling for the younger men; she loved the young ones. All that vodka took its toll. Roberta started to let herself go.

She wasn't in the Communist Party. She loved her life. She loved good people, people who were intelligent. And she helped me out. There was a time when I was broke. The party had abandoned me, and I didn't know how to go on. Roberta simply went to the Red Mill restaurant with little cards advertising my place.

In the evenings, students from the Technical University, railway employees, and bricklayers all came to the Eisenacher Hof for a glass. The students were smart and spirited; they would play the piano and raise a ruckus.

EISENACHER HOF DRESDEN A 21 BEHRISCHSTR. 9 RUF 5 34 82
INHABER MAX UND JOHANNA KRAUSE   SÄCHSISCHE LANDESKREDITBANK KONTO NR. 228924

SPEISEGASTSTÄTTE – GEPFLEGTE BIERE – 2 VEREINSZIMMER

Eisenacher Hof advertising header. (Estate of Johanna Krause.) *Translation:* Eisenacher Hof, Dresden A21, Behrischstr. 9, Tel: 53482 / Owners: Max and Johanna Krause; The Credit Bank of Saxony, Account #: 228924 / Restaurant—Specialty Beer—2 Clubrooms

Every Saturday and Sunday, the Eisenacher Hof was the place to be. The dancers from the Palucca School were still regulars. Later, during my court case, party leaders referred to them as whores. It was an absurd charge. Those dancers came to my place because they were young and wanted to hear some beautiful music.

Some customers were put off by the fact that I was Jewish, but they came anyway because they were curious. After spending one evening at my place, they usually couldn't resist coming again. They accounted for about half of our customers.

One day Roberta approached me. "You have to help me, Johanna. My mother has died and I'm very unhappy. Can I make it on my own?" Roberta's mother had played a big role in her life. I spoke to a pastor about burial plans.

Another time Roberta confided that she had fallen in love with this fellow. "But how am I going to earn money in the future? You know what? I still have a bust of the emperor in my cellar." We took the bust of Emperor Wilhelm II to an antique shop. "Nah, I can't buy that off you," the antique dealer said. "Maybe someone else will take it." We went from store to store. In the end, the emperor returned to the cellar and stayed there until Roberta's daughter and her boyfriend used it in some sort of caper.

At any rate, Roberta pawned everything she owned to support her daughter, who was very grateful. Her decline started with the arrival of the Russians. In the beginning she had a svelte figure, but after a while she let herself go and got fat. But her voice was as good as ever; it went straight to your heart. When she sang there was hardly a person in the place with dry eyes. She was a person with great passions, an artist, and

Max (*with beret*) and Johanna hiking in the Harz mountains, 1950s. (Estate of Johanna Krause.)

that's what killed her in the end. That and all the vodka ... gulp, gulp, down the gullet!

At some point Mrs. Steglich, who lived in Roberta's apartment building, came to me and said that Roberta was very sick. She had been ill for some time. "I can't come right now," I told Mrs. Steglich. "Perhaps another time." I was preoccupied with my booming business in those days. The party needed me to make business for them.

Roberta died soon after. I felt sad and guilty. How could I have let her down like that? Why hadn't I gone to her? I could have managed a visit. But that's how life is sometimes. Still, I brooded about it at the funeral and much later as well. Today there's no one left who remembers those times.

Mrs. Steglich was a classy lady, but every four weeks she was plagued by the moon. During every full moon, she would lie drunk in bed. She was so ashamed of that, I can tell you. After a couple of days, she'd be herself again and go back to telling the most marvellous stories. Roberta, Mrs. Steglich—these were the people who were my friends. We had only a few friends from the time before the war. That's how it is in the restaurant business. You have only a few friends, but it goes deep. We were friends with a few people from the art scene, and many Jewish friends came to the restaurant. Sometimes the Jewish community held large events in our clubroom.

One time my husband bought chickens from a Jewish man in preparation for an event. "You go have a rest," he said to me that evening. "I want to do everything myself." He went to work and then had a nap himself. At some point, the neighbours woke him up. "Something's burning at your place, Mr. Krause!" The house didn't burn down, but the chickens weren't so lucky. I have no idea how he did it, but Max managed to serve half-decent food that night.

One of my Jewish friends, Henriette Messner, predicted that the restaurant would be my undoing. Henriette was a very intelligent woman. She was a regular customer and often sat at the bar thrilling others with her wit and charm. She came by her prediction through talking to the other customers. I had gotten to know Henriette at the synagogue. She was from Löbau. She spent the night at our place following a big Jewish holiday event in Dresden one day, and after that she often stayed with us rather than making the long drive home.

During the war, Henriette had been in exile in France. She had a son named Otto. Her husband was not Jewish, so theirs was a "privileged marriage" too. One day Henriette called me on the phone and urged me to come to Löbau. "I can't just leave Max in charge of the restaurant," I said. "He's an artist, not a businessman. They'd take him for a ride." Still, I got Max to talk to her on the phone. "Oh Max, let Johanna come," she pleaded with him. "Three days. You can handle it."

"Okay, but you have to tell Johanna yourself."

Back on the phone, I tried to get Henriette to tell me what was going on. "I can't tell you on the phone," she said, "but it's important, Johanna, I'm begging you...."

So I went. My dachshund, hidden in a large bag, accompanied me. Max had given me the little dog after I learned that the Nazi doctor who cut me open and took my child had also sterilized me. A dachshund is something small and warm to hold on to. Over the years, I have had many dachs-hunds.

Henriette's husband picked me up from the train station. "You'll find out everything when we get to the house," he said.

The table was set. Henriette had prepared a wonderful kosher meal. For every course there was the appropriate wine, just like in France. After the meal, she came out with it.

"Johanna, we're all leaving here."

I was shocked. "What did you say?"

"As a Jew, my son would have it too hard here. We have no future in this country. We're leaving."

And then she named all the Jews—except one man who was illiterate and could barely scribble his name—who planned to flee the country. She listed all the people who came to our restaurant, people I knew. One of them was named Meier. "Just three days ago I heard Mr. Meier give a political speech," I said. "Everyone applauded, and it wasn't like he's about to take off."

"But Johanna, he had to do that; it's a *fait accompli*. I advise you to do the same. I can see what's been going on at your restaurant. We'll never see each other again if you don't come. You'll thank me for it later."

"But Max is communist," I answered. "He believes in the ideals. It's his whole life. He won't do it. I won't leave without my husband. And I can't just drop everything from one moment to the next. No way." Many of the East German Jews were leaving at that time, and I was the first to refuse the offer to go.

After our talk, we enjoyed the rest of the evening. Henriette wanted to give me something valuable. I looked over her things. "I don't want your stuff," I told her. "You should take it with you and sell what you don't use. You know very well that you're going to need money to get settled."

Not long after, my good Henriette was gone. I don't know how she did it exactly; it was so many years ago. I never saw her again.

At that time, the chairman of the Dresden Jewish community was still alive. His name was Leon Löwenkopf, and he was a wonderful man. I had great respect for him. He too fled to West Berlin.

Then I was summoned to the Stasi. They asked where I had been those three days. Before my interrogation, Max had instructed me not to give them an address. "If it goes badly," he had said, "say you don't know anything. Keep it to yourself." I told the Stasi that I had been at my sister-in-law's place in Leipzig. My husband's sister was a Nazi. "Because of Johanna's and my political position," he said to her, "your children could study medicine. If you screw things up for us, I'm going to expose your past." Her husband's past was terrible, so she didn't hesitate to cover for me. She was a good mother even though she smothered her two sons so much that one of them didn't marry until he was sixty! She was a real bourgeois dame.

The Stasi asked about more than just my whereabouts. "Mrs. Krause, why have all the Jews left? Did you know anything about that?"

"This is the first I've heard about it," I said. Of course, I knew about it. "I can't believe they're all gone. Mr. Meier just gave a speech not long ago. That's not possible."

They tried to ferret out some connection between me and Mr. Meier, but they couldn't prove anything.

"Did you know that a Mr. Silberberg is still here?"

Mr. Silberberg was the illiterate man who could barely scratch out his name. "You'll have to talk to him about it. It's none of my business. I don't want to get involved. I have nothing to do with it all."

I don't know if they believed me, but Max and I were so well prepared that they couldn't prove anything. They would have had to beat me to death before I would have talked. I was still physically fit and could keep my head. From everything I had suffered already I knew exactly how to survive something like that. They couldn't do anything to me. I had been well trained by the fascists.

That was our first run-in with the authorities since 1945. It would not be our last.

13   My Mother Died in Theresienstadt

After returning to Dresden, I learned that my mother had died in Theresienstadt. Being married to my stepfather had protected her during the Nazi period. She worked as a cleaner for the Henrietten Society, an old-age home for Jewish women. The women living there were like prisoners. They could no longer go out, and they weren't allowed to hire "Aryan" cleaners from the outside. There weren't many Jews left and the women couldn't do all the housework themselves, so my mother applied and started to clean for them.

She saw and experienced a lot there. The Hitler Youth often came by to make sure that the women were home. "Oh, my daughter has a tall blond husband," my mother would tell the women. "He's Aryan." I told her to stop spouting all this "Aryan" nonsense, but she failed to grasp why she shouldn't.

During one of my visits, a resident said to me, "Your husband has so many Christian friends. We'd like to get hold of some butter. We'll give you something for it; the Nazis will take everything from us eventually anyway." At first my husband refused their offer, but it didn't matter because I had already told them we would do it. They gave us wonderful things—books, extra food, clothing. Max was very worried because what we were doing could have earned us the death sentence if we'd been caught. But like other such things, it became a habit.

My mother started keeping a diary. The entries would be along the lines of "Mrs. Sara so-and-so received this or that for a book or a piece of silverware." (All Jewish women had to add "Sara" to their names.) Or she'd write, "Max Krause did this or that and delivered something." The diary worried me.

The old-age home for Jewish women where Johanna's mother worked. (Dresdner Hefte 29, no. 12 [1994]: 69.)

At one point, I did not see my mother for three days. Right away I knew something was up. I went to police headquarters to ask about her, "Your mother is on a transport for Theresienstadt," they said.

My mother had to wear the yellow star. When her husband died, she was no longer in a privileged marriage. After an eight-week period of mourning, she was picked up. I rushed home. "We have to go tomorrow," I told Max, "and see if the apartment has been sealed." I spent a sleepless night terrified that the Nazis would find the diary and see our names in it.

The next day we went to Stephanienplatz 4. My mother lived in our old apartment on the top floor. The roof was not the best but some tenants would venture out on it to get some fresh air; one time a dog belonging to a tenant on the fourth floor slipped and fell off the roof. Baroness von Rabenstein was still living in the building. She was the neighbour who had notified the authorities when I was young and my stepfather beat me so badly.

The Nazis had indeed sealed the door to my mother's apartment. We went at noon because most people were at work then. We took pains to make sure that no one saw us. First we rang the bells on the top floor; no one answered—perfect. Then we went to a neighbour, Mrs. Nassthal, who had the extra key to my mother's place. She had been lame for thirty years and was totally dependent on her husband. He was a barman and always under the influence, but they never fought about it. She was always happy to have him back.

As a young girl, I had helped Mrs. Nassthal out. I would get her things from Sternberg, a big arts and crafts shop, so she'd have something to occupy herself. When she went to the bathroom, her old wooden wheelchair always made a racket. I would go to her when I heard that noise, sit her on the toilet, help her up again, and wipe her bum. I did everything for this woman because she was such a good person, and she was so grateful. She was grateful to me her whole life.

Mrs. Nassthal told us what had happened. "It was shameful. Three days ago the bell rang and there were two men standing outside. Your mother was still in her nightclothes. At first she just closed the door on them. "If you don't open the door now, we're breaking it down," they threatened. During all this, it seems she fetched the five-mark coins. Then she opened the door. She acted like a hellcat; she was in shock. The men chased her up and down the stairs—and she was still in her nightclothes! Suddenly I heard a clinking sound in my mailbox. Then my doorbell rang. I stayed calm and listened. "Did Mrs. Samel drop something in your mailbox?' the men asked. 'Yes, she did,' I answered. 'That was my key. I'm very sick and lame, and so Mrs. Samel had my key.' "

That Mrs. Nassthal was very clever.

She gave me a wallet. It contained the five-mark coins I had given my mother every so often to buy herself something with. To think that she had had the presence of mind to throw those coins into the mailbox so the Nazis wouldn't get them! I still have the coins and the wallet today. I had tried to get Mrs. Nassthal to keep the money. "You're always so short of money," I told her. But she refused, and that's why I still have those five-mark silver coins with Hindenburg on them.

"Mother Nassthal," I said to her now, "my husband is going to open the seal with his magic hands. If anyone comes, take your wheelchair and head for the bathroom. I'll know from the sound of the chair that the coast isn't clear."

The apartment had not been searched yet because the seal was still on it—that much I knew. My husband had brought tools from home and he painstakingly made dots around the seal so that he could later return it to its original position. Then he removed the seal.

Nothing had been taken from the apartment. They must have seen that my mother was not well off. The only thing of value was a mirror with a golden baroque frame that the ladies from the old-age home had given her. Now I could hardly run around the city trying to sell this mirror, so I decided to give it to Mrs. Nassthal. "If you sell it off, you'll earn lots of money," I told her. "No, I'll keep it as a reminder of your mama," she said. Being a tailor, Samel had three sewing machines, and so I gave her one of these too.

The only things I took were the diary and an old Nazi flag that my mother had hung on the wall because she thought it would help save her. What lunacy. My mother was totally apolitical. She spent her whole life looking after people and never really understood what fascism was. She was unassuming and satisfied with what she had—in other words, completely different from me.

Finding the diary was not easy. We had very little time because people would soon be returning from work. And it's in just such moments that the devil plays a trick on you. So I searched and searched the apartment, and in the end I found the diary under the mattress. The mattress was a filthy mess, crawling with bedbugs. I took the diary and the flag, and we rushed home. If we had been caught, we would have been done for.

I tore the flag to shreds and then Max and I buried it in the Great Garden, Dresden's big central park. I read the diary and was enraged by entries like "My son-in-law Max Krause received such-and-such on day X." I mean, it couldn't be clearer. Her stupidity could have earned Max the death penalty. We burned the diary right away; it didn't tear easily but luckily we had coal ovens.

Handwritten declaration, dated June 17, 1951, by Olga Rascher (concentration camp co-prisoner) describing how Johanna's mother died in the Theresienstadt concentration camp. (Estate of Johanna Krause.) *Translation follows, page 110.*

Statutory Declaration

Johanna Samel was transported to Theresienstadt concentration camp with me on January 11, 1944. We shared the same room in the camp on Jägergasse 15 and then on the 1st floor of the same building until Mrs. Samel had to go the hospital at the end of February 1945 where she died on March 1, 1945. I often visited Mrs. Samel in the hospital, and I paid her my last respects there.

We all liked Mrs. Samel, who was so hard-working, and we were all very sad that she had to die so near the date of our liberation.

> Mrs. Olga Rascher (born Schwarz)
> Goethestr. 31, Radebeul
> Victim of Fascism #...
> June 17, 1951

Text of Olga Rascher's declaration.

After her arrest, my mother was held at police headquarters for two days. By the time I got there, she was already en route to Theresienstadt. She was sent with the transport of January 11, 1944. It was during this time that Horst Weigmann tried to free his mother and other Jewish women from the same police station. He pretended that he was Commissioner Schmidt but was exposed and murdered by the Nazis at the police prison. His mother, Toni Weigmann, was put on the same transport as my mother.

Prisoners in Theresienstadt were allowed to receive packages weighing one kilogram or less. When Max sent my mother a package, he was ordered to appear before the Gestapo. "Why would you, an Aryan, send a fruit loaf to a Jewish pig?" they asked. Max held his own. "She is not a Jewish pig; she's the mother of my wife." They responded by beating him severely. They also confiscated the package (no doubt keeping it for themselves), and so my mother never heard from us.

When I returned to Dresden after the war, I learned about what happened to my mother from two women, Mrs. Bauer and Mrs. Rascher. There were no gas chambers in Theresienstadt, but despite that my mother had a dreadful end. She became ill and was hospitalized. She received inadequate treatment because there was a lack of medicine in Theresienstadt. When the doctors had to amputate her leg, she was fully conscious; there was no morphine or anything else. So in addition to the camp, she had to experience all of that pain. And on February 28, 1945, she died.

Grave of Johanna Samel in the Theresienstadt concentration camp memorial site, July 1996. (Photo by Carolyn Gammon.)

A few years ago, I had the opportunity to visit my mother's grave. Mr. Aris from the Dresden Jewish community showed me the Gestapo files indicating when my mother had been picked up.

I am glad that I saw her grave.

Mass grave site at Theresienstadt concentration camp memorial site, 1996. (Photo by Carolyn Gammon.)

ARCHIV PAMÁTNÍKU TEREZÍN

DES VERSTORBENEN – ZEMŘELÉHO

Beschau – Ohledání	Absterben – Úmrtí	Beerdigung – Pohřeb	Personaldaten – Osobní data		
1945 28.2.	NH V-129 Samberger	Hans Wille	20.12.1882	XVII/10	615
	– V-130 Reimann	Ernestine	28.12.1892	AE 4	316
	NH V-128 Hartog	Adele	13.11.1869	XVII/7	1602
	NH V-127 Ledermann	Hedwig	20.7.1868	I/96	13114
	NH V-126 Zombosco	Charma	6.12.1866	IV/4	340
	NH V-125 Klein	Mary	27.12.1869	XXVII/1	267
3.3.	*NH V-135 Samel	Johanna	23.1.1874	E/10	411
	NH V-131 Rosenberg	Alexander	28.11.1888	VII/20	224

Official list of deaths from the Theresienstadt concentration camp. Johanna's mother, Johanna Samel, is listed on March 3, 1945. (Estate of Johanna Krause.)

14 "That Johanna Krause—She's Dangerous"

After a few years of relative calm at the Eisenacher Hof, our problems with the East German Communist Party began. First I turned down their offer to run another restaurant. I didn't want to give up the Eisenacher Hof.

Then the time came when Max stopped telling me about the party meetings he attended. "What's going on?" I demanded after one of those meetings. "Are you trying to hide something from me?" He tried to put me off. "You have so much on your plate, Johanna. You have your business to take care of."

But I persisted. "That's it. I'm not going downstairs at all today. You can run the restaurant yourself. You have to tell me what's going on. Now!"

"I'm to go to Berlin for retraining," he finally admitted. "You're supposed to follow me. We are to give up the Eisenacher Hof."

Now that we were all supposed to be model comrades, there was no place for a privately run business. Many restaurants in our neighbourhood were to be closed down, but mine was the first to go. It didn't seem fair that many of the others were allowed to stay open much longer.

I asked Max what he had said when the party told him their plan. "That I wanted to discuss it with you first," he replied.

I was angry.

"You're a coward if you think that plan is reasonable. I returned to Dresden to help you out. We built this restaurant together, and I helped nurse you back to health. When I returned after the war, it looked like you were on your death bed. I lay beside you, and you were sick, so sick I almost couldn't take it. And now you're considering such a thing?"

"I wasn't considering it at all, Johanna," he protested. "I'm very sad that they want to do this to us. We worked so hard for the Eisenacher Hof.

I'm not going without you, that's for sure. What would you do in Berlin anyway?"

That was the party's first diplomatic effort to make our lives difficult, to wear us down by separating us. I ran the Eisenacher Hof as usual, but they kept working on me. They noticed that I had withdrawn from the party. I stopped going to the regular meetings, and that was frowned upon. I worked day and night. I was quick as a weasel and kept everything in my head, but I had no time for the party. I couldn't do both; it was either my business or the party—and my husband handled party activities a lot better than I did anyway.

I couldn't just close shop; my customers were hungry. During those times, the neighbours and their children were regular visitors. Because of the party, my restaurant had food. Whenever there were leftovers, I cooked up a big pot for the children. At the bottom of the pot there was always a residue of thick stuff. At noon the kids sat around the big pot eating this stuff—they called it Plinzen. I wrote out little name tags with "Horst" and "Fritz" and so on so each child would have a portion and... down the hatch! "Don't eat so much!" they would say to each other. There was nothing to eat back then; a loaf of bread cost a hundred marks. But I and the two girls who helped me didn't go hungry, thank goodness. My husband was entitled to a ration card because he was a labourer, and I received more because I had been in a concentration camp.

Years later when we lived on Schlossstrasse, a tall and well-built young man appeared on our doorstep. "Good day, Mrs. Krause," he said. I didn't know who he was at first. He explained that he was one of the children who had eaten the Plinzen from the bottom of the pot. "I'm a farmer now," he went on. "Today I may have enough to eat, but I've never forgotten you. I've told everyone in our village about those days." I remembered him. He had three siblings, and his mother had come to me in tears, asking for something to eat. Over the years, many of the people I helped during that time have sent me letters of thanks saying, "My dear Frau Krause, may God bless you."

After Max turned down the party's offer to go to Berlin, strange things started to happen around us. But the party still needed him. They were looking for an honest type who would never accept a bribe, and that's how my husband ended up working at the housing office for nine years. One

Johanna with her dachshund Wuschel, one of her workers (right), and the children who ate the Plinzen, at the Eisenacher Hof circa 1955. (Estate of Johanna Krause.)

time a butcher told Max that he wanted an extra room because it was nearly impossible to get rooms; there was still rubble everywhere. Max turned him down. "I have to give rooms to people who have none at all," he explained. The butcher wrapped up an extra large package of meat. When my husband saw the package, he realized what was going on. "Listen to me," he said, "I'm sending my colleague to you. I can't deal with this at all."

Max never took bribes. He was too ethical for that. In fact, he was generous to a fault. I could never have left him in charge of the restaurant; in half a year, we would have been over our heads in debt. He was an artist, not a businessman. But the people from the party wrecked his career. He just wanted to paint. In fact, right after the war he rejoined the state artists' association. But instead of painting, he had to work in the restaurant. Painting would have been much better for his lungs than working in a smoke-filled restaurant.

Strange things were starting to happen at the restaurant. One day a married couple came in. Actually, they only pretended to be married. I knew the man by sight. The woman had bad manners; she was a drinker and was always picking her nose. The man ordered a drink and something to eat. She had nothing but drinks. At the end of the evening, I approached them. "Could I ask you to settle your bill, please. It's closing time."

"You Jewish pig!" the man yelled. "You just want to take my money."

My husband wanted to beat him up. I called the police, but they didn't come. I never found out if the couple were paid to do what they did. I just don't know.

On another occasion, a neighbour came to me with some disturbing news. "There are a whole bunch of swastikas at your place. I was just over there. Didn't your girls see them?" My helpers slept at our place in the large apartment we got from a man who moved to West Germany. I went right over and, sure enough, there were swastikas scrawled on the walls and swastika flags flying. I immediately filed a complaint with the police. It was no use, of course. Most of the people in positions of authority were former criminals, Nazi criminals.

Then I had a run-in with one of my waitresses. As we were about to do our accounts one evening, she said that her money was gone.

"That can't be," I said. "It's impossible because you just cashed some in."

"Well, it must have been stolen."

"And who would have done that?"

"I really have no idea."

I knew she was lying. "I'm going into the office," I told my husband. "You can tell her you're going to call the police, but in the meantime I'm taking her on myself."

I called her into the office.

"You should know," I said, "that I was a waitress myself when times were very bad and I lived with my husband in the big studio apartment. So you can't pull the wool over my eyes. I've been in this business for years, and I know for a fact that the money is not gone. Give it to me, and I'll consider this incident forgotten."

"I don't have it," she insisted.

"So you want to fight, do you?" I said more sharply. "I don't recommend it because, in the end, I'm going to tear you apart. I mean I'm working with thieves here!" Suddenly I reached out and grabbed the money she'd been hiding from me.

"Okay, now let's count it up," I said, "and whatever's left over is your dust." That's what we called tips, "dust." After the money had been counted, I said to her, "Okay, that's that. But don't do it again. See you tomorrow."

I never saw her again. The next day I was alone, and the restaurant was jam-packed. Finally, my husband arrived after doing his work for the housing committee. "It's about time you got here," I said to him. "You've got to work in the kitchen. I'm at the end of my tether." Most of the customers I served that night ended up helping me. In the midst of all the chaos, Max said to me, "Listen Johanna, our new party secretary is here. He's been waiting half an hour."

"Well, he can keep on waiting just like all the others."

After a while, I did go to him.

"Yes please, what would you like?"

Then everything on the tray I was carrying—glasses, plates, all of it—fell onto his lap. I recognized the Nazi who had tried to kill me.

I bolted to the office. Max hurried after me. "Is that any way to treat our new party secretary?" he demanded. "Aren't you ashamed of yourself?"

"For God's sake," I said, "that's no party secretary for me. That's Herbert Ossmann, the killer!"

"Johanna," Max argued, "you're having some sort of concentration camp flashback."

But I launched into him.

"That man is a fascist! He's the one who tried to throw me out of Germany. I know the man. Remember, I was with him for two whole days. He tried to kill me. There's no way I'm serving him!"

It was hard to believe that an SS man like Herbert Ossmann could end up being a Communist Party secretary. I suspected that he had been in a Russian prison and probably went to a Marxist-Leninist school there. Speaking Russian would have helped him secure this position in Dresden. As it turned out, I was right—but Max didn't believe me at first.

From that day on, Herbert Ossmann and the party tried to do me in. They came up with the most wonderful tricks. At closing time, midnight on the dot, there would be a policeman standing at the front entrance of the Eisenacher Hof. Sometimes my husband would open the door suddenly, and the police officer would fly through the door. The departing customers would laugh uproariously at the sight of the policeman lying on the floor.

At any rate, they made my life hell. They had to find something, and if they wanted to find something then they always did. They stuck together and slowly but surely put the screws on me. The party kept a file on me. Much later, with Freya Klier's help, I got my hands on that file and read the part where it said, "That Johanna Krause—she's dangerous. She must be gotten rid of. If not, we will be in a lot of trouble."

They kept me under observation. If I was guilty of the smallest infraction, I had to pay a fine. One time a woman asked if I could sell her a bit of coffee. "No," I said, "I can't do that because I have to sell by the cup, and I have to pay taxes on my coffee. Where would I get real coffee anyway?" But she begged me and begged me, and finally she offered to pay by the cup. Still, I refused.

She wasn't about to give up. "But if you charge me for so and so much powder per cup, then you know how many cups you've sold. There can't be anything wrong with that."

So I sold her the coffee, although it was forbidden. The woman did not report this to the police, but she must have bragged about it to her friends because word got out. There was a court case, and I fainted in court. All the harassment and dirty business was taking its toll.

On top of that, the party members stopped coming to the restaurant. Only the artists still came. They helped me out. They brought me far more business than the comrades ever did. And they treated me better too. If I so much as asked the party members if they wanted something to drink, they would groan and say I was bothering them.

Even with the support of the artists, there were long stretches during the winter when the place was empty and I would sit there by the coal oven. At some point, I told my husband that I was working on a plan to turn things around. "From tomorrow onwards, you're going to see the old Johanna Krause again!" I said. The next day I went to the university. I asked a man there if they had a student cafeteria. When he said no, I made him an offer. "I'll take on about twenty of your students. The food is not expensive. Come and try it out." It wasn't long before he contacted me, and the students started coming.

One day a student named Karl Jever came into the restaurant. He lived around the corner and worked part-time as an optician. At our place he became acquainted with Erika Schneider, a very nice woman who lived with her parents. She liked to frequent the restaurant because she thought so highly of Max. They shared a love of literature. Erika read books like War and Peace and the works of many Jewish writers. She and Max would exchange books.

So it was at the Eisenacher Hof that Erika and Karl met. Things were going well for Karl. In addition to a girlfriend, he managed to acquire five businesses, a car, and a piece of land. It was through Karl that I got to know a truck driver named Herbert Hammer. At first glance, Herbert didn't seem a bad fellow; it's just that he was always dirty and would soil my white tablecloths with his dirty hands.

One day Karl and Herbert came into the restaurant. Max was away performing some task for the party. He would take care of the elderly, organize parties, and the like. He didn't want money. He would use any bonus he received to throw a special party for the old people with lots of food and all the extras. On one occasion, in recognition of all the work he'd done, they invited him to attend an event with Dresden's mayor.

On this one day, Karl wanted to have a going-away party because Herbert Hammer was leaving for the countryside. They asked me if they could have a case of beer; they would return the favour by giving me and my two girls pullovers. Their offer was very tempting. I had a seamstress who would make new clothes out of old ones for a bit of food, and so I was always well dressed. But I hardly had anything to wear.

"I don't know," I said. "Max isn't here. Is it really okay?"

"Really, Johanna, of course it is!" Karl was a party member after all. "If you prefer, you can buy bedsheets from Herbert for one hundred marks, and he'll use the money to buy a case of beer and a bottle of schnapps. Herbert doesn't need bedsheets in the countryside; in the countryside, people help each other out."

"Are you sure everything's above board?" I asked him one more time.

"Of course it is," Karl said. "I wouldn't be here if it wasn't."

Shortly after I received a letter from the state prosecutor stating that I had bought stolen bedsheets. When I got that letter, I fell so ill that I could not appear at the first hearing.

So, the two men had sold me stolen goods. And they were not the ones hauled into court—I was! All of Dresden turned out to see me in court, even the ones who had broken into the restaurant at some point. "Where's Krause? We want to see her." But I had been to a doctor I trusted, and he and another doctor confirmed that I was not in any condition to appear at the hearing.

It turned out that Herbert Hammer had stolen the goods from the train station. In the end, he was convicted. Twenty-five people had bought goods from him. A colleague of mine who had a bar nearby bought children's clothes and sixty zippers. As far as the police were concerned, we were receivers of stolen goods. An old Nazi and now party member named Heller sorted out who was to come to trial and who was not. I was accused along with a few others. Karl Jever and Herbert Hammer had sold all sorts of things to all sorts of people.

In the end, everyone was released except me. The people who had bought the most stolen goods were in high positions; they were released. The woman who owned the bar received a suspended sentence.

All told we had three lawyers working on my case. "Mrs. Krause," they said, "you are surrounded by rats. We can do nothing for you. We can try but we know it will not work. The court has already decided, and it would cost us our livelihoods."

I was sentenced to four months prison in Dresden.

15 Jail for Me, Jail for Max

In 1958, it started again.

"Your wife will be back in two or three hours," they said to Max when they picked me up. I thought I'd be back soon too, because there were twenty-two testimonials in my favour before the court. But then these testimonials suddenly "disappeared"; Herbert Ossmann & Co. were going to use any means at their disposal to take my restaurant away from me.

The testimonials had been written by friends who were high up in the Communist Party ranks. But even these people were warned that their children would encounter problems or they would lose their livelihoods if they ever tried to support Johanna Krause again. When my lawyer asked to see the twenty-two testimonials, he received a letter some months later stating that they were "not to be found." Not only that, the letter said, but "the authority who dealt with this case is no longer working." My lawyer couldn't do anything more. The deck was stacked.

I was held at police headquarters for eight weeks awaiting trial. During this time, Herbert Ossmann and two Sector Control Police (former SS and SA men) stopped by regularly to check up on me. The guards were decent to me. They knew something fishy was going on.

In what was clearly a show trial, I received a four-month prison sentence for being in possession of stolen goods. The sentence was handed down on the anniversary of Max's and my wedding. I was incarcerated in the Dresden prison on Schiessgasse where I had already been imprisoned by the Nazis for "defiling the race." In prison, I couldn't take it anymore. For four months, I did nothing but cry.

Johanna in the 1960s. (Estate of Johanna Krause.)

There were five of us in the same cell: one young woman who was very political and very pregnant, an orthodox Catholic who prayed with her crucifix day and night, two other political women, and myself.

After eight weeks, shortly before Christmas, I had a breakdown. I ran to the door of the jail and started banging on it with my hands and feet. "Open up," I cried out, "or there's going to be trouble!" I was totally out of control. The door opened, and there stood a doctor surrounded by guards. "I want to be shot with my husband," I continued yelling. "Just like the brother and sister Scholl!"

I started to order people around. In the end I was crowing like a rooster. I could have earned lots of money doing that. My crowing sounded so realistic—and so loud!

Anyway, I put on quite a show. The prison doctor must have felt sorry for me because he gave me two morphine injections. Then my female guard arrived. She was nicknamed Mona Lisa because of the part in the middle of her hair. Another guard was called Pretty Bosom because she had such pointy breasts.

After I recovered from the injections, Mona Lisa returned me to my cell. "That's it—she's going to the bunker for that," one of my cellmates predicted.

I had become incredibly fussy about the prison food. I couldn't get anything down anymore. My nerves were shot. If things didn't change, I would probably end up in a psychiatric ward.

One day Mona Lisa insisted on taking a walk with me. Once we were in the yard, she turned to me. "Krause, can't you pull yourself together? Your enemies—Heller, Hauptmann, and Ossmann—want to see you locked up with the loonies. Please be reasonable." That advice could have cost Mona Lisa her job. But I just couldn't stop crying. My eyes were swollen. "I can't do it," I said. "I just can't stop crying."

"I'm going to put you in a cell with a librarian," Mona Lisa finally said. "I think you'll like her. She likes to sing, and she laughs a lot. Maybe she'll cheer you up."

And so I was put in a cell with Mrs. Tobias. Her parents had owned a large engineering firm in Dresden, Weissen Hirsch. Mrs. Tobias kept her hair in a bun, and she wore a simple white blouse and blue skirt. She was in jail because she had been caught smuggling gold to the West in preparation for an escape. Later she applied to leave and did, in fact, make it out.

In prison, I was not allowed to receive mail or have a change of clothing. I was treated no better than a serial killer. That's what really got to me and made me cry so much. I used to take things in stride, but prison life turned me into a nervous wreck. Max was not allowed to visit me, and so I had no idea what problems he was having with the Eisenacher Hof or the People's Solidarity Association. Around this time, he was expelled from the party and his "victim of fascism" status was revoked.

I was supposed to get out by Christmas, but shortly before my release date one of the guards informed me that Mrs. Tobias was being released instead.

I was shocked. "But I've done my time," I protested.

"That's true," the guard replied, "but it's those three men again. You're getting out after New Year's."

"How is that possible?" I asked.

"Mrs. Krause, you've already made it through the worst," she consoled me. "You can survive another few days."

I made it, but I could no longer eat. "Herbert, please don't give me so much to eat," I told the other guard. "I'm getting fat."

When I was finally released after New Year's, the report about me stated that I had been a model prisoner in most respects. Unfortunately, I was very sensitive and my non-stop crying had gotten on everybody's nerves.

Max picked me up after New Year's. Once we were home, I gave into my exhaustion. "You stay right here in bed," Max said. "I've already arranged things so we don't have any debts."

A few days after my release, Max and I were summoned with great authority to a meeting attended by all the party bigwigs. At this meeting, I was expelled from the party and we learned that the Eisenacher Hof was to be turned over to the People's Solidarity Association. A meeting of neighbourhood residents to deal with the motion to close my restaurant had already been held. They had prepared for the meeting by spreading lies about the Eisenacher Hof in the local papers. I have been very cautious about the media ever since. At that meeting, Ossmann—the new head of the People's Solidarity Association—had addressed the residents.

"Dear comrades, we want to close the Eisenacher Hof. It's a bad place. It is frequented by whores and the clientele is the lowest calibre. In its place we'll have the People's Solidarity Association. You'll be able to buy a cup of coffee for fifty cents, and there will be cultural events as well as opportunities to knit and do needlework, among other activities. It will be a great success. Does everyone agree?"

"Yes!" the residents yelled out. They clapped their hands in appreciation of Ossmann. This former SS man who had shot and beat Jews to death. This swine who had hounded and almost raped me.

At the end of the meeting, they all sang "The Internationale." My salvation came later on, when Ossmann was caught and convicted in a huge fraud case. If not for that, he would have destroyed me.

So, the Eisenacher Hof was shut down and turned into a veterans club controlled by the People's Solidarity Association. The piano mildewed. We sold the chairs for three-and-half marks. They took our belongings— the restaurant supplies, the schnapps, everything—and dumped them outside in the rain. My husband managed to salvage sixty blue and white plates. I still have them today.

Luckily, we did not have any debts. But one man tried to cheat us. He sent us a huge bill from the place where we ordered our beer. Max checked our books and then confronted the beer salesman. "What bill are you talking about?" he demanded. "Here's the paid bill. You have the duplicate." Obviously, this fellow had thought, Johanna Krause is in dire straits and so I'll just kick her while she's down. But he was the only person who tried anything like that.

Three days after we started packing up, they picked us up again because supposedly we were planning to escape. My husband sat in front of his old Erika typewriter and wrote a letter to Hilde Benjamin, the much-hated GDR justice minister who had had been married to a Jew (Walter Benjamin's brother). Max asked if she could help. He informed her that we had taken nothing from our bank account. Our claim was verified.

One time I was held at police headquarters for a week. I went into a crying jag when they didn't let me speak to Max. If they had, he would have told me not to worry; they were just up to their old tricks again, and I would soon be released. I never saw a cent of compensation for that unjust detention.

Then we received a letter telling me to appear before a psychiatrist at Schillerplatz to assess my "disabled" status. In 1946, I had been determined to be 50 percent disabled. I had never tried to get my status changed because I didn't want to stick out. Max accompanied me. "You're in no state to go alone," he said.

The head doctor reviewed my files. There was a long silence and then suddenly he banged his fist on the table. "I'm a doctor, not an informer! This woman is sick. She can keep her status!" He turned to my husband. "Try to work on getting your wife a higher status," he said. "You can take her home now." That was so good of him. He was a doctor, not a swine. I never saw the letter that the party sent him, but this time they did not achieve their aims.

Finally, we had some peace. But after everything that had happened, I did little but sit at home on a chair and refuse to eat. "If you don't eat, you're going to die," my husband scolded me. "You're worrying me no end. Your body can't take it like it used to. You're not so young anymore, and you're not going to just bounce back. You have to pull yourself together."

But I couldn't. I didn't look for work. I just sat around the house and did nothing but cry. Max cooked for us. I felt the loving warmth he was offering, but I still didn't know what to do with myself.

My husband had arranged for groups of people from Dresden-Blasewitz to eat at the Eisenacher Hof. The Saxony restaurant association had always held their meetings in Dresden. There was one restaurant manager called Neuberfeld. One evening he came to our home. He tried to speak to me, but I didn't answer him.

"I've had enough! Pull yourself together!" Max shouted at me.

"Don't yell at your Johanna," Mr. Neuberfeld said. "She's going to come and work for me. You can pick her up every day and have a drink at my place. The drinks are on me, and I get a good barmaid in return."

We accepted his offer. It was wonderful to be working again. Mr. Neuberfeld would often bring me a little something to eat. He treated me like a small child. I was there only a short while because word got out that I was back on the job. I was approached by Mr. Staschko, the first director of restaurants in East Dresden. "Mrs. Krause, I need you," he said. "I really need your services."

The Schillergarten had been in private hands up until that point. It was four thousand marks in debt, a considerable sum in those days. I was to run the restaurant on behalf of the Southeast branch of the HO—the organization of state co-op restaurants. I received a letter stating that I would be managing the bar in the Schillergarten and the beer garden during the summer. "Mrs. Krause is to have full responsibility," the letter went on, "and she is to be exempted from the back-breaking work."

I was in business again. I was in control of everything. I could order the supplies, hire whom I wanted. My husband helped me build the inventory. The HO would check my inventory along with my wine cellar. (I had a wine cellar so I could see exactly what was in stock.) Soon the Schillergarten was back on its feet, and I managed to avoid any debts. Once when I was away, there was a break-in; no supplies were taken, thank God.

When the place was closed for renovations, I worked at the restaurant on Schillerplatz. One time the coffee machine crashed down on top of me. My whole face was black and blue. "It figures such a thing would happen to you," the boss said. The man who replaced me couldn't handle the job. Then a woman took over, and the coffee machine fell on her too. So the boss saw it really wasn't my fault.

In 1960, for the second time, my husband was charged with libel of the state. People said that he was going around claiming that the Commu-

Johanna working in the Schillergarten, circa 1970. (Estate of Johanna Krause.)

nist Party was full of SS people. I had been in jail when the first charge was laid. That's how they tried to take our business from us; they had found out that my husband owned the licence. They didn't follow up on that charge, but now they were trying it again.

This time the East Dresden district court gave Max a nine-month sentence for slander of state authorities. It all happened so fast. He was imprisoned in Bautzen II, and I visited him there. Then he was moved to the jail in Zittau. That jail was full of Sorbs (the Slavic people from Southeast Germany), and my husband, as a Silesian, was immediately accepted by them. Max was born in 1902, the son of a plumber. He was an accomplished locksmith and worked in the jail's tool room. The Sorbian prisoners appreciated him because he was intelligent and totally honest. If he was working with the other prisoners and a tool or something went missing, he'd call out, "Hand it over now! Out with it or I'll do a job on you until your teeth fall out!"

Max's steady nerves served him well in prison. On top of that, my husband was big and strong, and the men respected that. The male prisoners understood one another. I had not experienced this with the women.

After four months, Max's lawyer informed him that Ossmann has been arrested in Berlin. "We're going to reopen your case, Mr. Krause." After five-and-a-half months, Max was released and accepted back into the party. The charges against him were dropped from the records.

What had happened? Herbert Ossmann, by then the head honcho at Pentacon (a huge camera factory on Schandauer Strasse), had committed fraud to pay for his whoring around and his expensive holidays. He grew increasingly cocky. For instance, he'd haul out his old SS papers and show them off. He was working less and less and dressing to the nines. He beat his wife and cheated on her too. In the end, she got her revenge and told the police. In 1961, Ossmann was caught near Berlin—all of his SS documents packed in his suitcase—trying to flee to the West.

Comrade Friedrich, who lived nearby, stood under our balcony one day and called up to me, "Hanna, can I come up?"

"I'm not a comrade anymore," I said looking down from the balcony. "Stay where you are. I'm not letting you in."

"For God's sake, Johanna. I have something to tell you. Come on, let me in."

"No, I don't want any visitors, and don't talk to me as if we were still comrades. You're not coming in."

"Will you let my daughter in then? She was Ossmann's secretary, you know."

"Okay, she can come up."

The daughter told me that they had nabbed Ossmann just before he made it to Berlin.

As soon as I heard this, I went to the daughter of Roberta Förster-Frohberger and asked if she could write a letter to the authorities on my behalf. Shortly before his arrest, Ossmann had tried to evict me from our apartment. Max was still in jail, and I had learned at a citizens' meeting that I was to leave our apartment within three days. My furniture would have had to be put in storage, and I would have ended up in a damp Nazi basement apartment in Strehlen.

Three days. On one of those three days, Ossmann was arrested, and I got to stay where I was. It was like a fairy tale. If they had not nabbed him, I would not be alive today.

It was the luckiest day of my life.

Otto Griebel   A b s c h r i f t !
Dresden-N 54
Pillnitzer Landstr. 11   Dresden, d.25.III 1953

Nachstehend gebe ich folgende eidesstattliche Erklärung ab. :

Ich, Otto Griebel, gehörte seit 1923 derKPD und seit Gründung der
SED an, in denen ich als Funktionär immer tätig war und noch bin.
Während des Naziregimes bin ich Massregelungen aller Art ausgesetzt gewesen.
       Seit dem Jahre 1931 gehörte Max Krause, geb. am 17.2.1902,
meinem engeren Bekanntenkreise an, weshalb ich über seine politische
Haltung und über sein Schicksal genaue Auskunft geben kann. Dadurch,
dass Max Krause im Jahre 1933 in das gleiche Haus (Ostbahnstrasse
1a) in dem auch ich wohnte, zog, waren wir dauernd in engster Füh-
lung und verheimlichten als gesinnungsgleiche Menschen und Freunde
einander nichts. So las ich seinerzeit auch die Anklageschrift, die
seiner jetzigen Frau in Jahre 1933 vier Monate Gefängnis wegen
"Führerbeleidigung" einbrachte. Anfang 1935 wurde die Obengenannte
als politisch vorbestrafte ungarische Jüdin Landesverwiesen und von
der Gestapo ohne Pass über die tschechische Grenze abgeschoben.
       Um nicht wegen Passvergehens straffällig zu werden, kam die Lan-
desverwiesene illegal nach Dresden zurück, hielt sich einen Tag bei
mir auf, und wurde weiterhin von Max Krause verborgen gehalten, bis
ihr dieser ein ungarischen Pass verschafft hatte. Am ersten Oster-
feiertag 1935 brachte Max Krause sie mit Pass über die Grenze der
CSR zurück und versorgte sie von da an mit allem Lebensnotwendigem
trotz der grossen, damit verbundenen Schwierigkeiten und Gefahren.
Der unbedingt notwendige Schriftverkehr zwischen Beiden erfolgte
über meine Anschrift. 1935 reiste Max Krause wiederholt nach Prag,
bis es ihm gelang, von der CSR- Regierung den zu einer Verehelichung
notwendigen Dispens zu erwirken. Max Krause heiratete
dann seine jetzige Frau in der CSR trotz des schon in Kraft getre-
tenen Nürnberger Rassengesetzes am 21.X.1935 . Beide kehrten dann
nach Dresden zurück, wo sie beide kurz nach Weihnachten 1935 durch d.
die Gestapo wegen Rassenschande verhaftet wurden, und erst Anfang
Mai 1936 ihre Freiheit zurückerlangten. Es war Max Krause gelungen
den Ariernachweis des ausserehelichen Vaters seiner Frau beizubringen
Den Ausschlag zur Freilassung gab aber der Zufall, dass Frau Krause
in der jüdischen Gemeinde unter dem Frauennamen ihrer Mutter, nämlich
unter dem Namen " Pollack" eingetragen waren. Frau Krause führte
jedoch rechtlich den Mädchennamen ihrer Mutter, L i n d n e r.
       Ein Jahr lang liess die Gestapo das Ehepaar Krause in Ruhe.
Darnach wurde der Fall wieder aufgegriffen. Allein im Jahre 1937
hielt die Gestapo Max Krause mehrmals auf Wochen in der Bismarckst.
inhaftiert. In den folgenden Jahren wiederholte sich das immer wiede
Bereits 1937 war Max Krause aus der Reichskulturkammer wegen po-
litischen Unzuverlässigkeit und jüdischer Versippung ausgeschlossen-
worden. Max Krause litt seit seiner ersten Verhaftung, wie ich
beobachtete u. damals annahm, an chronischen Hustenanfällen, die sich
nach und nach verstärkten. Als Max Krause im Januar 1941 für
faschistischen Wehrmacht gepresst wurde, blieb er dort nur 3 Wochen
und musste wegen offener Lungen Tbc als untauglich entlassen werden.
Anfang 1942 wurde er nach der Lungenheilstätte Adorf i/V geschickt,
wo er sieben Monate zubrachte, blieb dann in Dresden weiter in
Pneumathorax - Behandlung. Trotz seines Krankheitszustandes wurde
Max Krause weiterhin von der Gestapo geholt.
       Da ich mich von 1947 - 1956 selbst nicht mehr in Dresden
aufhielt, verlor ich Max Krause aus meinem Gesichtskreis und er-
fuhr erst später von seinem weiteren Schicksal und all den Leiden
denen das Ehepaar Krause bis zum Ende des Naziregimes ausgesetzt wa
       Ich kenne und schätze Max Krause als einen entschlossenen
Antifaschisten und möchte hervorheben, dass nur wenige Menschen
soviel persönlichen Mut aufbrachten wie er und bin der Überzeugung
dass die vordem völlig intakte Gesundheit ax Krause durch die ca.
ausgesetzte Verfolgung und Massregelung durch die Gestapo in der
Nazizeit total untergraben worden ist, weshalb er einen ganz besonderen
Anspruch auf die Fürsorge unseres Staates voll verdient.

                        gez. Otto Griebel, Staatssekretär der BB?
                             für bildende Kunst Dresden,
                             Mitgl. Buch der SED Nr. 1.014.719

A letter, written under oath by the Dresden painter Otto Griebel, attesting to Max Krause's anti-fascist activities and persecution during the Nazi period. (Estate of Johanna Krause.) Translation opposite.

Otto Griebel   <u>D u p l i c a t e</u>
Dresden—N54
Pillnitzer Landstr.   11 Dresden, March 25, 1953

I submit the following statutory declaration:

I, Otto Griebel, have belonged to the German Communist Party since 1923 and the SED Party since it was founded, and I have always been active in an official capacity and still am. During the time of the Nazi regime, I was subjected to all sorts of hateful regulations.

Since 1931, Max Krause, born Feb. 17, 1902, has been part of my inner circle of friends, which is why I am in the position to make a precise statement about his political position and about what happened to him. Because, in 1933, Max Krause lived in the same house as I did (on Ostbahnstrasse 1a) we were in closest contact and, as we shared the same political views and were good friends, we hid nothing from one another. Therefore, in 1933 I found out the same time he did that his current wife had been charged with "insulting the Führer" and sentenced to four months in jail. In 1935, this same woman, as a Hungarian Jew with a previous political conviction, was thrown out of the country without papers over the border to Czechoslovakia.

So as not to break the pass laws, she then returned to Dresden illegally. She stayed with me one day and then was hidden by Max Krause until he could obtain a Hungarian pass for her. During the Easter holidays, 1935, Max Krause took her back over the border into the Czechoslovakia with the pass and obtained everything she needed to exist there despite the great personal difficulties and dangers this entailed. The necessary correspondence between the two was done using my address.

During 1935, Max Krause travelled numerous times to Prague in order to obtain the allowance to marry from the Czech authorities. Despite the fact that the Nuremberg race laws were already in effect, Max Krause married his current wife on Oct. 21, 1935, in Czechoslovakia. They both then returned to Dresden only to be arrested by the Gestapo shortly before Christmas 1935 for "defiling the race." They were able to regain their freedom by May 1936. Max Krause was able to secure papers to prove that his wife's father (not married to the mother) was "Aryan." That they were released from jail was also due to the coincidence that Mrs. Krause was not registered in the Jewish congregation records under her own name but that of her mother's first husband, "Pollack." Mrs. Krause, however, carried lawfully the maiden name of her mother, "Lindner."

For the next year, the Gestapo left the Krause couple in peace. Then they were attacked again. Max Krause was arrested many times and spent many weeks in the prison on Bismarckstrasse. In the following years, this pattern was to repeat itself. In 1937, Max Krause was expelled from the Reich Chamber of Culture because of being "politically unreliable" and "related to a Jew." Since his first time in jail, I observed how Max Krause developed a chronic severe cough that became worse and worse.

When Max Krause was pressed into fascist military service in 1941, he was released from duty after only three weeks as "unfit to serve" because he had full-blown tuberculosis of the lungs. At the beginning of 1942, he was admitted into the TB sanitarium Adorf i/V for seven months. Back in Dresden he was further treated for pneumothorax problems. Despite these health problems, Max Krause was repeatedly picked up by the Gestapo.

Because I was not in Dresden myself from 1943–45, I lost track of Max Krause and was only able to learn later of all the suffering the Krause couple went through until the end of the fascist regime.

I know and appreciate Max Krause as a resolute anti-fascist, and I must stress that few people showed so much personal courage as he did. I am convinced that Max Krause's health, which had been fully intact beforehand, was destroyed by the persecution under the Gestapo during the Nazi period. He has therefore especially earned the right to have full access to all the health care that our state offers.

Otto Griebel, Director of Students
at the College of Fine Arts, Dresden
SED Party member #: 1.014.719

16 The Years Grow Quieter

After Max got out of jail, he was rehabilitated by the party but still had great difficulty finding work. He would go to an interview and later receive a letter saying that the position regrettably was already filled. I continued to work for the HO, the state co-op restaurant.

One day I went to Max with an idea. "You know what? It doesn't have to be like this. You could go to the state theatre and work backstage moving props and whatnot. When they realize who you are and what you can do, you'll get a promotion. With your lungs you couldn't do that heavy work for long anyway."

So Max applied to the state theatre and accepted a position as a stagehand. The work was very hard. Soon he was transferred to the paint shop where the artists worked. There he helped create set designs. In fact, after only six weeks or so of working there, he won a prize for designs he had made for a swivelling music stand and rotating pieces of scenery. Then he was moved to the metal workshop on Ziehstrasse where he taught the apprentices. He was an art metalworker after all. He received awards for his teaching too.

My husband had an inborn talent. Actually, he was a bit lazy. In school, he exerted himself only when they threatened him with not getting an "A." His talent and brains were such that while another person could grind away at something and still not get it done, Max was always on top of things. He was born under a lucky star.

I returned to the Schillergarten after it was renovated. I worked there for nine years. During that time, I saw ten or so bosses come and go. Some were terrible. One of the worst was an anti-Semite. He tried to give me a rough time, but I always defended myself. "Okay," I said, "if you're going to fight with me like that then I don't want you to show your face in my wine cellar." Of course, I still got the blame if anything went wrong.

One of the students took over on my days off. I would give him just the supplies he needed to get through the day, and everything worked perfectly. I never took on a waiter if I wasn't sure of his honesty. This student was completely trustworthy. Unfortunately, he didn't remain in the business.

On one of my days off, the cellar was broken into. I went to the main office on Brennerstrasse and resigned on the spot. They looked around for a replacement, but the customers and other workers wanted me back. Someone from the head office approached me. "Mrs. Krause, please come back. As you know, there are frictions everywhere. The fellow who's given you such a hard time will treat you better from now on."

So that's how I ended up at the Schillergarten for nine years. During that time, I lived with Max at Eisenacher Strasse 42. If I had the night shift or worked evenings, I always had my cigarette money and accounts with me so that in the morning Max could help me with the books. In the winter I tramped through the snow, and in the summer I walked through the balmy night air. Fortunately, nothing serious ever happened to me; nobody attacked me.

Eventually we left Eisenacher Strasse because so many disagreeable people lived near us that we no longer had our peace of mind. In 1975, we moved to Schlossstrasse 1 where I still live today.

After leaving the Schillergarten, I went to work at the East Restaurant on Schandauer Strasse because we needed the money. The manager there weighed over four hundred pounds. One day she took a fall right in front of me. The head waiter called for an ambulance, and it took four men to carry her out. One of her legs became affected with gangrene and had to be amputated.

When I heard that, I panicked. "That's it, I'm gone." My colleague thought I meant I was off to the toilet, but I went to change and clear out my locker.

"Are you crazy?" she said. "You can't just leave the buffet!"

"Why not? I've done a good job here, and now I'm going. I can't get the image of that woman lying stiff on the floor out of my mind. I've had my fill of this place."

She tried to get our colleagues to persuade me to stay. But I was adamant. "Go back to your customers. How can you leave them alone? They'll say it's my fault. Get back downstairs."

They were panicking. "What are we going to do without you?" one of them said.

"One of you can take over the buffet," I replied. "Or get the woman who cleans the washroom for all I care. I'm leaving."

"You're so stubborn," someone grumbled. "If we'd known that you were just going to take off like this after working so long...." In fact, there had just been a celebration marking my twenty-five years of service. But it was over now. I was well over seventy years old.

I went to the office responsible for pensions. "I'm way past the age for getting a pension," I said. "Shouldn't I have started receiving pension payments five years ago?"

And so they started paying my pension.

My husband also worked into his old age, until he was blind. They didn't want to lose him. Even when he was blind, they still wanted him. "Max," they said, "you don't have to work. You just have to tell us what to do."

In those years when we still worked, we sometimes had the chance to go on holiday. We went to Grillenburg, which was lovely, and to Hiddensee. We travelled all over the coast of the Baltic Sea, in Binz and Sassnitz. One time we went to the Erzgebirge where we met some very nice people. I loved to go dancing!

Of course, every marriage has its problems, and sometimes our life together was not so exciting. We were together for forty-nine years. We married in 1935. Actually, my husband never wanted to marry. We could have stayed together as a common-law couple, but he had to marry me so that I could become German.

By the time we both retired, Max was already very ill. He had cancer, but he wasn't treated for it. For a long time, he went to Dr. Palme. He was a country doctor, and I really liked him. One time I took our little dachshund, Wuschel, with me to the doctor's. When I returned home, Max asked me where the dog was. "Oh my God!" I cried out. "I tied him up somewhere when I was shopping!" Then another thought occurred to me. "He must be at Doctor Palme's!" Max called and, sure enough, Wuschel

Johanna, Max, and their dachshund Wuschel in Binz on the island of Ruegen, circa 1960. (Estate of Johanna Krause.)

was there. Doctor Palme had just taken him on a walk to the park to do his business. With all that had happened to me, I had become somewhat forgetful.

Later we switched to a woman doctor, Dr. Schuhmacher. It took me some time to get used to her, but after a while we got along well. She was kind and hard-working. At that time, victims of fascism were legally entitled to immediate treatment. It galled the other patients that I could always just walk right in.

At one point Dr. Schuhmacher sent Max to another doctor, who diagnosed testicular cancer. He told me but kept my husband in the dark; he didn't want Max to lose hope. They gave Max some fruit, and he thought that was wonderful. In East Germany at that time, fruit was severely restricted. Whenever Max tried to give me some, I would brush him off because I knew that he needed it more than I did.

During Max's illness, a woman I had befriended at the sauna also helped out. She had dark hair with a part in the middle, and she was very thin. She was a good soul. She always indulged me in the sauna, brushing me from stem to stern. She was a Jehovah's Witness and tried to convert me at first. After a while she realized it was a lost cause, and we began a friendship that didn't involve religion. She took to Max instantly, visiting the hospital every day and keeping me informed about his condition. At that time, I was still working two days a week and so I couldn't go to the hospital so often. When I did get a chance to come in, I would ask her about his condition. "Yes, yes, he's getting better," she'd always say.

One time I arrived at the hospital just as they were giving bananas to the patients. Max didn't eat any so my friend was going to take them home with her.

"Hey, those stay here!" I snapped.

"But he's not eating them," she protested.

"Ah ha! So instead of trying to encourage him to eat, you're just taking them for yourself or other people!" Then I looked at Max and arranged the blankets and realized what was really up. Max was down to skin and bones. I blew up at the Jehovah's Witness because she had not been honest with me.

After three weeks, I took Max home with me. First I had to speak with the doctor. The Jehovah's Witness advised me to give the doctor a bottle

Johanna and Max, circa 1980. (Estate of Johanna Krause.)

of schnapps, which I did. Then my husband told me something that made me regret ever having given the doctor the schnapps. The doctor had allowed my husband to be transferred to another hospital for X-rays, injections, and radiation wearing nothing but a nightshirt! The clueless nurse's aide didn't even bother to cover him up. The result of all this was that he contracted pneumonia.

I yelled the place down. The Bible lady showed up, and I ordered her to call a taxi right away. "We can discuss what happened between us later, but for now, I'm taking Max home with me." I had to sign papers acknowledging that I was taking him at my own risk. At home I wrapped him in a wool blanket made of camel hair. "Do you want to watch a bit of TV?" I asked. He smiled at me and his eyes shone. He had the most beautiful blue eyes. He was so grateful.

Soon Max was in so much pain that they almost ended up killing him with their injections of morphine, which were kept at his bedside. It was awful. Many people from the Jewish community came to his sickbed. Everyone loved Max. I would say he was better liked than I was. He had done a lot of good in the world, and they all knew it.

Toward the end, my friends had to help me get Max up out of bed. I was too small to do it alone. My good friend Helga was a godsend. She lived through it all, sleeping over at our place and doing everything she could to help out. She was so loving and really sacrificed herself for us.

Max died next to me in bed. It was a hard death. He could no longer speak or eat. I would hold a glass with a straw to his lips, and the best he could manage was a sip or two. "If you don't eat," I said to him, "then you'll die, and you can't just go and leave me alone." I also encouraged him to move a bit. At first he would try to give me a sign with his beautiful hands, but then he couldn't even do that anymore. He would just groan in pain.

"Try to be a bit quieter," I said to him one night. "We have to sleep."

And then he was quiet. Suddenly I realized that he had died. How could I have said what I did? On the other hand, how could I have known what would happen?

Deep down, of course, I had hoped that he would live a bit longer.

Helga washed and dressed him. When the nurse showed up, we just gave her the money; there was nothing left for her to do.

Johanna visits Max's grave in the new Jewish cemetery, Dresden, 1996. The inscription reads, "My beloved husband." (Photo by Carolyn Gammon.)

In 1982, I buried Max in our Jewish cemetery. That was an honour as Max was not Jewish. The Jewish community supported my decision because he had always protected me. I bought a stone made of Swedish marble and made sure everything was done properly.

17 At the End of Life

After Max's funeral, I was so worn out that the doctor said to me, "Mrs. Krause, it would be the best for you to be around people again." So for a few days I moved in with the fat woman who managed the East Restaurant. She was so happy to have me; she didn't want to let me go. After that the doctor prescribed a stay at a health resort.

The head doctor at the health resort asked me why I was still wearing black. "It's my duty to wear black for a year," I replied. "I just can't go around wearing a white blouse."

"Wearing black will not improve your health," he said. "That's why you're here, isn't it?"

So I bought myself a white blouse. The men at the health resort were all real buddies and very nice to me, but I didn't get along with the women. I kept my distance from the women.

Shortly after I left the health resort, my beloved friend Helga Hartung died of cancer. It was another devastating blow. She was pure gold to me. We had gotten to know one another at the synagogue. She was interested in Jewish music. Her husband was an organist in a church. She saw me in the synagogue and thought to herself, I'm going to become friends with her.

Actually, Helga had a thing for women even though she was married and had two children. She and her brother had a large property in Dresden, Weissen Hirsh. She invited me to her place, but in the beginning I didn't go. Then she wrote to me because I had given her my address. One time I went to a store to buy bed covers and it occurred to me that Helga lived nearby so it would be easy to pay her a visit and see what her place was like. Still, I hesitated. Making new friends has never come easily to me.

Johanna with her friend Helga Hartung in Johanna's apartment at Schlossstrasse 1, in Dresden in the 1980s. (Estate of Johanna Krause.)

When I did visit Helga, she was living with a female companion. This woman was lame, and Helga took care of her. The friend was very jealous of me. She wanted Helga all to herself because Helga cared for her like a mother from sunrise to sunset. At the same time, Helga ran about doing errands for me; she picked me up from the HO restaurant every day and carried my bags for me. It didn't seem quite normal, but I appreciated her because she was very well educated. Her father had been a dentist.

Helga backed off when she noticed that when it came to relationships we operated in two different worlds. Still, she continued inviting me and my husband. We would drive over to her place, and Max would rest in a lawn chair in her large backyard. I didn't have to worry about cooking on Sundays because she had everything prepared. First we would have coffee and cake and then supper outdoors in the backyard. She was a first-rate housewife.

When Helga became ill, I visited her in the Friedrichstätter hospital. It was so dreadful in that hospital. I packed a large bag full of juices to take to her. By the time the number 2 tram arrived at the last station, I was no longer able to carry the bag by myself. I just stood there and waited. Soon a young woman on a bicycle came by and offered to help. "I'm a nurse at the hospital," she said. "I'll put your bag on the back of my bike and just push it."

"You have been sent by the angels," I said.

At the hospital, I told Helga she was going to get better. "But I can't visit you that often," I added, "because it's so far."

"Why on earth are you carrying so much?" she asked. "I can't drink all that."

"You're sick so you have to drink a lot," I replied. "And these are good juices, full of vitamins."

"Okay, okay, I'll do what you say and drink them all," she said with a laugh.

Some time later, I received a letter from her children. I raced to the hospital. She was lying there and I didn't recognize her. There were all kinds of tubes sticking out of her, and I couldn't see her beautiful blue eyes. That wasn't my Helga. She was too weak to speak; she could only nod her head.

I confronted the doctor and made a huge fuss, like I'm wont to do. "What have you done to my friend? I was here not long ago, and she was talking and able to go for walks. I'm going to come every day now." She had been moved from a big double room into a ward.

"What can I do?" the doctor said. "When the next bed is free, she can go back to a double room. You can't say I'm guilty of anything. I can only do what's in my power."

The next time I visited, Helga looked beautiful. It had never occurred to me before that a dying person could look beautiful. I told her about my problems with the Communist Party. "Why do you bother with those boneheads who have it in for you?" she said. "Just be who you are and leave all that stuff alone."

"I'm not getting anywhere with my rehabilitation. I've been fighting for that for eight years already."

"If you want justice you have to fight for it, Johanna."

It was good to talk to her. I hoped that she would get better but deep down I didn't think she would. Her sons wrote to me that she was in a bad state, and that I should come one last time. During that visit, she told me that I had been her best friend. "You have such a big heart," she said.

Johanna with Carolyn Gammon (*left*) and Christiane Hemker (*far right*) at Weixdorf, 2000. (Photo by Carolyn Gammon.)

"You are not an easy person to understand, but I understand you." She was so loving to me. And then she died.

There were many people at Helga's funeral. She was such a well-loved person because she took care of everything and everyone. A friend of Helga's who had many cats was also there. They had visited Israel together. Helga had gone to Israel many times. During the service, I couldn't stop crying. I didn't hear a word the minister said. I just couldn't believe that Helga was dead. It seemed so sudden.

It was around this time that I rented a large walk-in locker at Weixdorf, the little forest lake just north of Dresden. I would take the number 7 tram out there and go swimming. After a while, I rented three adjacent lockers and used them to store a hot plate and a small couch. There was a picnic bench near the lake. I enjoyed many wonderful times out there, and the country air helped me recover. I was still swimming when I was nearly ninety. One time when I took a dip the water was only eighteen degrees. During a house call the next day, the nurse remarked that my blood pressure level was unusually good!

Johanna with one of the Russian veterans (who freed the camp) on the fiftieth anniversary of the liberation of Ravensbrück concentration camp, April 24, 1995. (Photo by Carolyn Gammon.)

My life changed significantly when Freya Klier contacted me through the Ravensbrück concentration camp memorial site. She had spoken to Eberhard Dentzer, one of the administrators there. Many of the books that have been written about Ravensbrück set out to describe what heroes some people were. "I don't want to hear about heroes," Freya said to Eberhard Dentzer. "I want to find a woman whose life took many twists and turns."

"I know just the one," he replied. "She's not very popular, but her life is really interesting and complicated. I don't know if it will work out. I've sent journalists to her before and she just turned them away."

One fine day Freya Klier turned up on my doorstep. She was standing there with a big bouquet of flowers and a box of chocolates. "I would like to speak with you," she said. Well, I couldn't just toss the flowers in the wastepaper basket. I'm not ill-mannered. So, I let her in. We clicked right away.

The Elbe River, on the border between Germany and the Czech Republic, where the SS man tried to drown Johanna in 1934. (Photo by Carolyn Gammon, taken during the filming of Freya Klier's 1996 documentary film, *Johanna: A Dresden Ballad*.)

Freya wanted to make a short film about my life. The film, *Johanna: A Dresden Ballad*, was a big success and was shown many times on TV. It was a success because I could just be myself. And when I'm myself, I can be very fiery. I wasn't afraid anymore. Freya was very proud of that.

After the film aired, men would come up to me and admit that it had made them cry. "Heavens, men don't cry!" I would tell them. The people in my apartment building were astounded by the film. Such a small, unremarkable woman…who could have imagined that such a story might be hidden there?

Of course, Freya Klier worked very hard to make the film happen. First she had to research everything, and many new details came to light. I read through my Stasi (secret service) files and found out many things I hadn't known before. I had already told Freya my whole story. When her research was over, she said to me, "Mrs. Krause, every word you've told me is the truth!"

Johanna with Freya Klier by the Elbe River on the German–Czech border, 1996. (Photo by Carolyn Gammon.)

Then we travelled to all the sites where fate had taken me—to Ravensbrück, Plan bei Marienbad, and other places in the Czech Republic. We went to the former factory where I had done slave labour. I showed Freya the corner where I used to leave my bag of laundry for the women to wash for me. While we were there, a man approached us. "What are you doing here? Filming is forbidden."

"Please excuse us, but I did forced labour here as a Jew during the war."

"In that case, go ahead and film."

I asked if I could speak to the boss who used to work there. "She's dead," he replied, "but I could fetch you someone who knows about that time." I turned down the offer. I wasn't interested. The main thing is that we got to do the filming.

The film could easily have run three hours, but Freya honed it to a perfect twenty-eight minutes. Even at three hours, I think the film would have appealed to people, and even then not everything would have been included. Whenever my film is shown, the people become very animated and those who know me say, "That's Johanna all right—feisty to the end!"

Freya Klier and Johanna in Mühlhöfen (where Johanna survived the death march in 1945) during the filming of *Johanna: A Dresden Ballad*, 1996. (Photo by Carolyn Gammon.)

Freya Klier is a wonderful person. I value this woman because she is incorruptible. You have to get to know her and be on the same wavelength and despise fascism. There are not many of her ilk.

All my life I have hated and fought against narrow-minded people and fascists. I hated them in the past and I hate them still today. As Freya wrote in her letter to the Gauck office (which administers the archive of the Stasi files), "I have never known anyone who hates fascism as much as Johanna Krause."

Freya came with me to the synagogue and filmed there. That made people in the Jewish community uneasy. They felt a bit ashamed that they hadn't helped me out over all those years. But that's human, all too human. I don't hold a grudge against anyone. I was an unimportant person. Why should they have helped me out? If I had been well educated or in some sort of high position, maybe things would have been different.

Thanks to Freya Klier's tireless research, my conviction was eventually overturned and I was rehabilitated. In the Stasi files, she found documents

Johanna with Christiane Hemker (*middle*) and Carolyn Gammon (*right*) in Johanna's apartment, Schlossstrasse 1, on the occasion of her ninety-second birthday, October 23, 2000. (Photo by Carolyn Gammon.)

indicating that I was to be eliminated because Ossmann and others thought I was too dangerous. She took the information to a lawyer. At first he wouldn't show up at set appointments. Then he told her that time had run out and my case would no longer be considered.

But Freya was not about to be put off. She went over the lawyer's head and met with a government minister. "I've gotten to know Mrs. Krause," she told him, "and I'm not going to watch her be beaten down. I've studied her case and I know that something went terribly wrong."

"Go to the state lawyer," he suggested. "He's in charge of all that."

She went to the two state lawyers and then the state court, and in the end I was rehabilitated. My criminal record from the East German times was finally erased.

After the fall of the Berlin Wall, I attended the events held at the Ravensbrück memorial site. Eberhard Dentzer invited me. "Johanna, we need you here," he said. "There were many lesbians in the camp, and you are

Johanna visiting her mother's grave at the Theresienstadt concentration camp memorial site, Czech Republic, 1996. (Photo by Carolyn Gammon.)

one of a few who are open enough to talk about this and to tell everyone how lesbians in the camp behaved and what their fate was."

"That's not so hard," I replied. "Surely you can find someone else."

"We don't know anyone better than you," he said. "How should I put it? You have a big heart and understand all different types of people. You know what I mean."

So I said yes because he was a friend of mine. At one of the events, I met Carolyn Gammon. Over the years, she has been very supportive, accompanying me to various memorial events and Jewish high holidays. She sat beside me at that first event held at Ravensbrück. Some of her questions were a bit strange; I couldn't answer them all.

It was through Carolyn that I came to visit my mother's grave in 1996. A friend of hers knew someone at the Theresienstadt memorial site. Connections are everything. I had been there before but had been told that I would never find her grave. This time I found it—a stone with her name,

Johanna during an interview in November 2000. (Photo by Dietrich Flechtner.)

Johanna Samel, and her dates. Finally, I placed the stones I had brought with me from Israel on her grave. I was oddly comforted by the fact that she lay here, halfway between Hungary and Germany.

In recent years, I've been spending more time with young or middle-aged people. I don't get along with old people. I noticed that the last time I was in the hospital. They put me in with a bunch of seniors. One rattled her teeth all night, another groaned incessantly, and still another talked non-stop nonsense.

The next morning I confronted the head doctor. "You have to get me out of here. I can't take these old people anymore."

"But Mrs. Krause, you're the oldest person here."

"Be that as it may, I don't feel like it. And I prefer the company of younger people."

I have given many talks to young people over the years. "My name is Johanna Krause," I begin, "and I'm from Dresden. I'm going to tell you about my life as best as I can. I am not like you. I never had the chance to study, to attend high school or college. But I think we will understand one another all the same." They all applaud and yell out encouragement. I feel that all-important connection. Then I continue:

The fascists murdered over 92,000 women of different nationalities, whether through epidemics or by shooting, gassing, starving, beating, or torturing them to death. These women were from France, Poland, Belgium, Czechoslovakia, Holland, Romania, Austria, Norway, Spain, Denmark, Russia, and the Ukraine.

Where once the gas chambers stood there is now a memorial stone with an eternal flame. The sites of terror—the narrow alley between two walls where prisoners were shot to death, the ovens of the crematorium—can still be visited today. One can also see the paths that prisoners under torture built up out of the swamps—the so-called Street of Cinders constructed from the ashes of burned bodies.

I remember that the smell of burning flesh poisoned the air. For hours we stood with bare feet in wooden clogs in the cold awaiting roll call. For months all we had to eat was a ladle of soup made from leftover potato peels discarded by the SS. We yearned for even just a little bowl of red beet soup.

Typhus, phlegmon, dysentery, freezing to death, the flu—these were our constant companions. During the day, we were tortured by the SS; at night, it was the lice and vermin. Even for the children there was no pity. They were sent, without exception, to the gas chambers—I mean in particular the Jewish children.

I had to carry heavy stones in the quarry up a hill and back down again. I had to clean out the latrines. I had to sort the clothes of children who had been murdered. I had to sweep the streets of the concentration camp. Our salary was to be beaten.

And as hard as it is for me to say, there was no solidarity in the camp for the Jewish prisoners. That is why I have always had problems with the former prisoners, and especially the political ones. That is why we always rub each other the wrong way.

At the end of my time in the concentration camps—Ravensbrück, Retzow bei Rechlin, and Neurolau bei Karlsbad—there was only one thing left: a death march. Only two women besides myself survived this hell.

It is a miracle that my dear husband and I survived this dreadful time, that we lived to tell about it.

Never again fascism and war. In all the schools and universities, in the churches, and everywhere else, we want to live and work in friendship. Our goal of peace is not a utopia. One day all of humanity will reach out a hand in equality.

When I was born I think a guardian angel must have peed on my head. This angel stuck with me and got me out of the most improbable situations. It wasn't my cleverness or intelligence that saved me: it was my protective angel and good instincts.

Yes, I had very good instincts. All my life, I fought and fought and fought again. I've been fighting the Nazis for decades. Actually, all I've done is fight fascism. And to think I'm just a small, unimportant woman.

That's just the way it is.

Appendix and Acknowledgements

Carolyn Gammon

It was March 1994 and I had been in Germany for two years when I came upon a notice in a Berlin magazine about a weekend seminar at the Ravensbrück concentration camp memorial site. Until then I had to forego such interesting seminars because my German was just not good enough for me to participate, but finally on this weekend I decided to go.

Growing up in Canada, I learned about the Second World War from a Canadian perspective. My mother's first boyfriend had been killed in the war, and this or that relative had fought. Every November 11th, on Remembrance Day, the veterans would march and we would lay wreaths at the local war memorial. But Europe and the realities of war seemed far removed. I had heard of the Holocaust and the concentration camps, though I could probably have named only one: Auschwitz. Then, while I was doing my M.A. in Literature and Creative Writing at a university in Montreal, I joined a politically active student group that was engaged in the struggle against racism and anti-Semitism. Alongside Jewish friends we learned some history, held seders where stories written by survivors were read out, and organized workshops aimed at fighting anti-Semitism. Moving to Germany to live with my Afro-German partner sensitized me to similar issues, but still, nothing really prepared me for that weekend in March 1994.

I had never been to a concentration camp memorial site. I had never knowingly met or spoken to a Holocaust survivor. I had a lot to learn about the workings of fascism. Arriving at Ravensbrück for the first time, I remember the shock—almost like a fist to the stomach—that the concentration camp buildings literally began where the village ended. Despite my education in Canada, I must have still harboured the belief that most Germans didn't really "know" what was going on. And yet from the shores of Schwedt Lake where the ashes were strewn from the crematorium, you could see the village church and hear its bells. The trains bringing prisoners had arrived in the village; the prisoners had then been marched through town to the concentration camp. When I later learned that a Siemens factory had been built nearby for the explicit purpose of exploiting the workers of Ravensbrück, any remaining illusions I might have held vanished: atrocious crimes against humanity had been committed a mere stone's throw from "civilization."

I remember meeting Johanna Krause for the first time. She was the honoured guest and witness to the events of the time, invited by one of the memorial site organizers, Mr. Eberhard Dentzer, who became her good friend and supporter. When I entered the room where the thirty participants had gathered, Johanna was already seated. The chair beside her was empty. Perhaps the German women present were too respectful or too shy to sit beside her, but I, in my friendly Canadian way, went right up to her, offered a handshake and a smile, and introduced myself. She responded warmly and said I should sit down beside her. We started talking, and it seemed there was an automatic affinity. I learned later that I had a bit of an advantage in that Johanna reserved a special place in her heart for foreigners! When I said I was a writer, she replied, "So that's it—my husband was a painter." And so we had another affinity.

At one point, Johanna expressed her concern that she wasn't up to the challenge of the seminar: "There are so many intelligent people here!" I assured her that she undoubtedly knew more than all of us put together.

The remainder of the weekend, we barely parted. Arm in arm we walked with other participants through the memorial site museum. "That red triangle," Johanna would comment, "that's just what I had to wear." At the crematorium she said, "You could smell burning flesh night and day." She spoke about her suffering and about the hard truth that Jewish prisoners did not enjoy the solidarity from other prisoners that communist survivors often reported—a distinctly unpopular view from the perspective of the former East Germany. At Johanna's side that weekend, I learned more about fascism, about the Nazi terror, and about survival than I had in all my thirty-four years.

There was a strange moment during the seminar when Johanna brought out all her documents: the number assigned to her and sewn onto the camp clothes, the triangle, the various passports and papers issued by the Nazis. Her suffering and survival had been painstakingly recorded and kept all these years. As Johanna stressed over and over how she had the documents to prove it all, it seemed as if we, the participants, were jurors in a court deliberating whether or not it really happened. Finally, someone broke the tension with the simple words: "We believe you." But Johanna was not with us. She was with an audience she had fought all her life, an audience that did not want to listen and did not want to believe. That stuck in my mind—the burden of proof resting on the survivors and how we, the next generations, must carry on that task.

At the end of the seminar weekend, I wrote Johanna a letter thanking her for her work. I was totally exhausted and full of admiration for a woman, then eighty-six years old (some fifty years older than myself), who had participated so fully at such a demanding event. My letter marked the beginning of a correspondence that lasted until Johanna's death in June 2001. The seminar weekend was the beginning of a deep friendship.

Johanna invited me to Dresden and I visited her in her bohemian quarters at Schlossstrasse 1, the heart of the old city. In the summer, we would go to Weixdorf. Johanna would swim in the little forest lake and recount, bit by bit, the stories of her life. She told me about her persecution during the communist times, about her faithful partner Max, about her present-day struggles. "All my life is a struggle," she often said.

In 1995, I accompanied Johanna to the commemoration of the fiftieth anniversary of the liberation of Ravensbrück concentration camp. Those five days at her side once again filled me with respect and love for this amazing woman. We heard other survivors speak, and we attended ceremonies and seminars together. Johanna gave interviews and met an Israeli delegation composed of Hungarian Jewish survivors. I watched as a Hungarian women, in a well-intentioned gesture, pinned a yellow star to Johanna's blouse. Johanna flinched inwardly but thanked the woman and managed to walk away politely before saying to me, "Please, take it off immediately."

One day there was a shortage of lunch packages. When I saw Johanna looking around desperately for hers, I realized how terribly difficult this memory work was, returning to such a place of pain. But Johanna handled

Johanna on the fiftieth anniversary of the freeing of the Ravensbrück concentration camp, April 1995. (Photo by Bettina Flitner.)

most situations with her customary sharp sense of irony. Chemical toilets at the memorial site were in short supply, and the lineups for these elderly people were up to ten minutes long. "I feel like I'm on the *Appelplatz* waiting for roll call," Johanna said. Wry wit and cutting truths were Johanna's hallmark. They earned her both love and fear.

I attended the annual Ravensbrück meetings with Johanna until poor health prevented her from attending. In 1996 I accompanied her to the Czech Republic for the making of Freya Klier's film. We stood on the bank of the Elbe River where the SS man had tried to drown her. We went to the site where she had survived the death march. We visited Plan bei Marienbad where she had recuperated for months after the war. In their determined search for the truth, Freya Klier and Johanna were kindred spirits. It was a miracle that the two of them had found each other and a wondrous experience watching them work together during the making of *Johanna: A Dresden Ballad*, that living testament to Johanna's extraordinary story.

On another occasion, I travelled with Johanna to the Teresienstadt/Terezin concentration camp memorial site, where she visited her mother's grave for the first time. It was a splendid day in June, and each grave in the vast yard had a red rose blooming beside it. The sight of Johanna placing on her mother's grave, stones that she had brought from Israel was tremen-

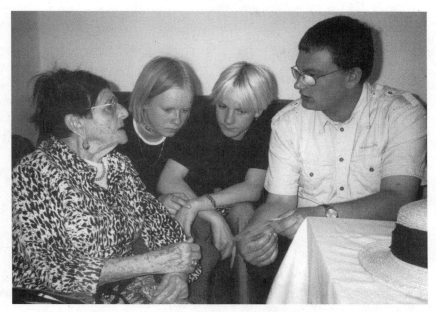

Johanna talks to young people during the opening of a concentration camp memorial site at Retzow bei Rechlin, May 14, 2000. (Photo by Carolyn Gammon.)

dously moving. It was one of very few times I saw her cry. "It's good to see her resting here," she said, "halfway between Hungary and Germany." At first I couldn't fathom how Johanna could take comfort in finding her mother's grave in a concentration camp. But then I realized that, unlike so many other survivors, she at least had a grave to visit.

In 2000, a new concentration camp memorial site was opened in Retzow bei Rechlin. (This former site of a German Luftwaffe testing centre in what is now the state of Mecklenburg-Western Pomerania had been transformed by the Nazis into a satellite camp for Ravensbrück.) Johanna, by then ninety-two and one of the only known living survivors, was asked to speak at the inauguration ceremonies. For an hour over a hundred people listened keenly as Johanna spoke in her direct and anecdotal manner about the conditions at Retzow and Ravensbrück. As always, Johanna worried that she had spoken for too long, but the pastor holding the umbrella to keep the sun off her remarked, "I could have listened to you another hour!" After the official gathering, Johanna asked, "Where's a video

Celebrating Johanna's ninetieth birthday in Dresden's old Jewish community centre, October 23, 1997. (Photo by Carolyn Gammon.)

recorder? The young people have to see my film." We all gathered in the local youth club and watched the film. Afterwards Johanna answered questions. The club was full of young people with pink spiked hair, platform shoes, and flared pants. They discussed everything with her, eager to learn more. And so Johanna put in yet another full day.

Our friendship also included simply enjoying each other's company. We walked around the Church of Our Lady and the old palace as it was being rebuilt. We went to the Great Garden and had cake at the Carola Palace café where Johanna had spent many an afternoon in her youth before it was "forbidden to Jews." We visited Max's grave or did a bit of shopping. Johanna's favourite place was Weixdorf. Into her nineties, she swam, picnicked, and breathed the forest air, exchanging her city stress for a few hours of peace.

After my son's birth, our visits included him. Johanna had to work on overcoming her jealousy; she would repeat the tragic story of her son being stolen from her by the Nazis. But she had a direct and loving way with children, and back in Berlin my son would look up at her photo and in his

Johanna dancing, at the age of ninety-two, in Dresden on Hanukkah, 2000. (Photo by Carolyn Gammon.)

toddler way say, "Hanna! Hanna!" So it seems she made an impression on him too.

Most often we just sat in Johanna's apartment, enjoying tea and delicious sweet rice with milk and cinnamon. As evening came on, she would drink the local beer I had brought her (Radeberger was her favourite). We chatted, looked at photos, and caught up.

Johanna's birthdays were always quite an affair, her tiny apartment overflowing with well-wishers. On her ninetieth birthday, which was celebrated in the Jewish community centre, she received so many flowers that she said she would have to open a shop. I was a guest at the annual Hanukkah celebrations in Dresden. My main duty was to try to stop Johanna from dancing too much!

The intergenerational friendship that Johanna offered me has been vital to my understanding of this country that I have chosen as my home. As she recounted her memories of her life and times, it was almost as if a century unfolded before my eyes. I have called Johanna my "grandmother in Germany," and yet somehow the word "grandmother" does not fit because Johanna was not old in the conventional sense of the word. She may have experienced a physical decline in her final years, but her spirit remained young, engaged in the world around her and always ready to take on a new challenge.

Over the years, Johanna often expressed a wish that her life story be written down so that future generations might be able to learn from it. I was slow to respond to this desire of hers because I feared turning our friendship into a working relationship. I also hesitated because German is my third language, and I knew that I would never be able to do the project alone. How could I possibly find someone who would be dedicated enough to take on such a challenging job, feisty enough not to be intimidated by Johanna's personality, and smart enough to measure up to her very high standards? But as the years passed and Johanna's health started to fail, I decided to take action before it was too late. In January 1998, I arranged for Freya Klier's film to be shown at a Dresden women's centre, with Johanna present to answer questions. The next evening I read from my novel-in-progress.

It was at these two events that I met Christiane Hemker. As an archaeologist with impressive academic credentials, she possessed a keen sense of history and was thus able to appreciate the importance of Johanna's story. I sensed from her straightforward manner that she would hit it off with Johanna, so I asked if she, as someone living in Dresden, would be interested in doing the interviewing. She said she would try, and then, after a period during which she got to know Johanna, the interviews began. They took place in Dresden and Weixdorf, and went on for about two years. It isn't possible to tell one's life story in a straight line, and so Christiane's task was to listen, to ask for clarification and details, and to find a unifying thread.

Following the last interview in July 2000, the job of transcribing and editing began. For this arduous work I organized funding in Berlin in order to hire qualified helpers. The first draft was presented to Johanna on her ninety-third birthday.

During the preparation of the second draft, Johanna checked the text for accuracy. Much of the challenge of recreating her life story derived from the fact that she was so exacting. Over and over during the process,

Johanna receives the draft copy of *Twice Persecuted* on her ninety-third birthday, 23 October 2000. (Photo by Ehrenfried Schaefer.)

she would say, "Every word must be true!" Yet how can one guarantee the truth of memories of such long-ago events? In the end, *Twice Persecuted* is Johanna's truth—told in her unique voice, and not intended to contradict (or even comment on) other truths. As the manuscript was read to her, she often spoke aloud, saying the same words simultaneously.

Twice Persecuted is the result of more than two years of intensive work completed with Johanna when she was in her early nineties. More than that, it is the culmination of friendships that began in the early 1990s and deepened over the years. Anyone who knew Johanna knows that she had a keen sense of people. She smelled dishonesty a mile away and was frank about pointing it out. That she trusted the two of us to produce a book about her life was an immeasurable gift of friendship.

I will conclude in the same way that Johanna and I always ended our telephone calls and visits: shalom, shalom!

Christiane Hemker

One winter evening in January 1998 I met Johanna. Freya Klier's film, *Johanna: A Dresden Ballad*, was to be shown, and Johanna Krause herself was to talk about her life.

When the film came to an end, the audience was quiet. On the women's faces you could see expressions of empathy and awe. I felt the same way. I looked at Johanna. She was a small, bent woman sitting in a wooden armchair. She was wearing black pants and a black leather vest over a colourful pullover. Her black hair was dyed and cut short. I looked in her face, ninety years young, and saw an energy and curiosity in her lively eyes. At that moment, I understood what it means to venerate someone.

I met with Johanna many times over the next few years. Most of the interviews took place in her apartment. In her tiny living room overflowing with memorabilia, she sat opposite me and told me about her life. On her voyage into the past, I accompanied her through all the phases of remembering, through all the emotions and moods that evolved.

There were times when the memories were too traumatic, and she couldn't go on. When that happened, I would shift the focus or even discontinue the interview. There were times when neither of us could go on. But when Johanna spoke of the Nazis, she did so with a relentless and unyielding fighting spirit. Her suffering, which lasted nearly a lifetime under various German political systems, had not broken Johanna down; it had made her even stronger, even more courageous and inventive. She never gave up.

Johanna was a woman of the 20th century. She was especially affected by the societal shifts and political events of the first half of the century. She liked to describe herself as small and unimportant and yet, in truth, her honesty, her courage and tenacity, and her profound sense of justice have inspired me and countless others. I believe that through this book she will serve as a model for future generations.

Johanna, you were never small and unimportant! I miss you!

* * *

This book came about through the efforts of many people. Our deepest gratitude goes to our friend, the late Johanna Krause. Despite often serious problems with her health, she never shied away from the rigours of an interview process that extended over a two-year period. She embraced this challenge with an admirable strength, never wavering from her belief that her life story could illuminate the times of persecution in which she lived.

We are greatly indebted to Birgit Michaelis, who not only transcribed many of the interview tapes but also took on the monumental task of editing the transcripts. Without Birgit's commitment, Twice Persecuted would not be the book it is today. We would also like to extend a heartfelt thanks to Ariane Kwasigroch, who transcribed the bulk of the interviews. We are grateful to Katrin Wolschke for proofreading the first draft of the German manuscript, and to Katharina Oguntoye for translating Carolyn's appendix text.

Karin Buron, Nora Goldenbogen, Freya Klier, Karin Meissenburg, and Eberhard Dentzer reviewed the second draft, and their insights and constructive criticism added much to the final version. Thanks also to Wolfgang Wünsche, who contributed photos from Johanna's estate, and the friendly staff at Ravensbrück Memorial Museum, who helped us to locate archival documents. Bettina Flitner contributed the wonderful photo of Johanna taken on the 50th anniversary of the freeing of Ravensbrück, and other photos were provided by Ehrenfried Schäfer and Dietrich Flechtner. A special thanks to Christoph Wetzel for his portrait of Johanna.

We would like to thank the student unions of the three Berlin universities (the Humboldt University, the Free University, and the Technical University) for the financial support we received for the transcribing and editorial work. We are grateful to Professor Wolfgang Benz of the Centre for Research on Anti-Semitism (Technical University, Berlin) for including this book in the Library of Remembering series.

We would like to acknowledge the contributions of the following friends and colleagues who gave invaluable assistance to the English translation of Zweimal Verfolgt / Twice Persecuted: Cathie Dunsford (Dunsford Publishing Consultants) and Karin Meissenburg (Global Dialogues Press) for providing editorial assistance and help with translation; Allison Brown, also for help with translation details; and Liselotte Neumark Doverman and Elizabeth J. Doverman for their devoted and in-depth German-English editing. A big thank-you goes to Sarah Robertson for her precise final edit.

Without generous funding from the Hans Böckler Foundation (www.boeckler.de), a Düsseldorf trade union association that funds socially progressive projects, *Twice Persecuted* might never have been published. We thank the Hans Böckler Foundation in the name of Johanna Krause and with all our heart. Their support shows the level of commitment in Germany to carry on this very important Holocaust memory work.

We would also like to thank Marlene Kadar at York University (Toronto) and Brian Henderson and all the staff at Wilfrid Laurier University Press (Waterloo, Ontario) for bringing Johanna's story to the English-speaking world.

You have all contributed to granting Johanna's last wish that her story be told after she was no longer here to do so herself.

—*Carolyn Gammon* and *Christiane Hemker*
Berlin, Dresden

Johanna: A Dresden Ballad
a film by Freya Klier

A 28-minute documentary film in German (with English subtitles) that summarizes the life story of Johanna Krause.

Review in a Saxon newspaper:

"The film does not attempt to explain but leaves the telling entirely up to Johanna. This gives it a forceful authenticity and dignity. The scenes are selected sparingly. Documents and photographs add the historical accent. And the camera lens avoids all sentimentality..."
Sächsische Zeitung

The DVD can be obtained by contacting:
Edition "Nach-Lese," M. Scheibner
Email: edition-nach-lese@web.de

Further information: www.freya-klier.de

LIFE WRITING SERIES

In the **Life Writing Series**, Wilfrid Laurier University Press publishes life writing and new life-writing criticism in order to promote autobiographical accounts, diaries, letters, and testimonials written and/or told by women and men whose political, literary, or philosophical purposes are central to their lives. **Life Writing** features the accounts of ordinary people, written in English, or translated into English from French or the languages of the First Nations or from any of the languages of immigration to Canada. **Life Writing** will also publish original theoretical investigations about life writing, as long as they are not limited to one author or text.

Priority is given to manuscripts that provide access to those voices that have not traditionally had access to the publication process.

Manuscripts of social, cultural, and historical interest that are considered for the series, but are not published, are maintained in the **Life Writing Archive** of Wilfrid Laurier University Library.

Series Editor
Marlene Kadar
Humanities Division, York University

Manuscripts to be sent to
Brian Henderson, Director
Wilfrid Laurier University Press
75 University Avenue West
Waterloo, Ontario, Canada N2L 3C5

Books in the Life Writing Series
Published by Wilfrid Laurier University Press

The Life Writings of Mary Baker McQuesten: Victorian Matriarch edited by Mary J. Anderson • 2004 / xxii + 338 pp. / ISBN 0-88920-437-3

Seven Eggs Today: The Diaries of Mary Armstrong, 1859 and 1869 edited by Jackson W. Armstrong • 2004 / xvi + 228 pp. / ISBN 0-88920-440-3

Love and War in London: A Woman's Diary 1939–1942 by Olivia Cockett; edited by Robert W. Malcolmson • 2005 / xvi + 208 pp. / ISBN 0-88920-458-6

Incorrigible by Velma Demerson • 2004 / vi + 178 pp. / ISBN 0-88920-444-6

Auto/biography in Canada: Critical Directions edited by Julie Rak • 2005 / viii + 264 pp. / ISBN 0-88920-478-0

Tracing the Autobiographical edited by Marlene Kadar, Linda Warley, Jeanne Perreault, and Susanna Egan • 2005 / viii + 280 pp. / ISBN 0-88920-476-4

Must Write: Edna Staebler's Diaries edited by Christl Verduyn • 2005 / viii + 304 pp. / ISBN 0-88920-481-0

Food That Really Schmecks Edna Staebler • 2007 / xxiv + 334 pp. / ISBN 978-0-88920-521-5

163256: A Memoir of Resistance by Michael Englishman • 2007 / xvi + 112 pp. (14 b&w photos) / ISBN 978-1-55458-009-5

The Wartime Letters of Leslie and Cecil Frost, 1915–1919 edited by R.B. Fleming • 2007 / xxxvi + 384 pp. (49 b&w photos, 5 maps) / ISBN 978-1-55458-000-2

Johanna Krause Twice Persecuted: Surviving in Nazi Germany and Communist East Germany by Carolyn Gammon and Christiane Hemker • 2007 / x + 170 pp. (58 b&w photos, 2 maps) / ISBN 978-1-55458-006-4